Starting out with CACTI

Neobuxbaumia tetetzo in southern Mexico

Starting out with CACTI

Prickly plants with flowers ranging from tiny to flamboyant

David L. Jones
B.Ag.Sci., Dip. Hort.

Contents

Epiphyllum 'Blackamore'

Hatiora rosea 'Regina'

Preface

My first cactus, given to me at the tender age of eight or nine, was a Peanut Cactus in a tiny terracotta pot. Intrigued as I was by the unusual spiny growths and amazed at its ability to survive dryness and neglect, I was truly astounded by the incredibly beautiful flowers that this novel plant could produce. I managed to add to my collection of cacti over the years, but then other plant groups took precedence, although I still maintained an interest in cacti. Much later in life, while living in Canberra, the interest in cacti was renewed, largely due to the influence of the late John Spencer of Goulburn. While in Canberra I managed to amass a reasonable collection, specialising in those that were frost tolerant. On retirement, this collection was moved to Kalaru, a near-coastal region in south-eastern New South Wales that throws up different horticultural challenges to those of Canberra. The survivors from Canberra mostly thrive in their new environment supported by many newcomers. Many of the hardier cacti are grown in a special section of the garden, others in pots. Epiphytic cacti have also gained precedence.

Cacti have an ardent following of dedicated enthusiasts in most Australian states. They are obviously very efficient in water use and well suited to cultivation in many parts of this dry continent. I hope that this introductory guide, which is a relatively simple introduction to a limited range of cacti, will promote them even further and encourage a wider range to be grown. Emphasis is placed on the more easily grown species and I have also treated epiphytic cacti as a separate group. They hold a special fascination for me and need to be grown differently from the terrestrials. Many epiphytes are surprisingly easy to grow with spectacular flowers, often verging on the flamboyant. Hopefully this book will promote their popularity. In all some 300 species and numerous hybrids, or cultivars, are discussed and illustrated in colour.

Keeping up with botanical nomenclature is a special challenge with cacti and I have chosen a standard path to follow for this book (see page 15). I have consulted the literature in an attempt to keep up to date but detailed molecular studies are regularly showing up the errors of past classification systems, even at the level of plant families. I have also included a glossary to assist with technical terms and a list of books dedicated to cacti.

Echinocereus pentalophus subsp. *procumbens*

ABBREVIATIONS

alt. altitude
cm centimetre
m metre
mm millimetre
sp. species singular
spp. species plural
subsp. subspecies
var. variety

Ferocactus pilosus

Part One
INTRODUCING CACTI

GETTING STARTED

Cactus plants (plural cacti or cactuses) are an intriguing group of dryness-tolerant plants that are grown by dedicated enthusiasts in many countries. Botanists place them in the Cactaceae, one of the most remarkable of all plant families containing some 1800–2000 species in about 90 genera. Essentially plants of the New World (an exception is *Rhipsalis baccifera* that has been spread out of the usual cactus range by birds), cacti range from Canada through the USA to Central America (also islands of the Caribbean region) and South America (south to Patagonia), and extending onto the Galápagos Islands.

Most cacti grow in the ground as terrestrials, but the family also includes highly modified epiphytic species that grow on rocks and trees. Ground-dwelling cacti can be found in a range of habitats in temperate and tropical zones, extending from the coast to areas well inland, and from low elevations near sea level to the arid slopes of mountain ranges at more than 4000m alt. Biting cold winters and warm to hot humid summers must be endured at these latter elevations. In parts of the USA, some species of *Opuntia* and *Mammillaria* are able to withstand arid conditions as well as seasonal snowfalls.

Terrestrial cacti exhibit a tremendous range of size, shape and growth features. Plants can be solitary, developing just a single growth, or spread by basal offsets to form clumps and mounds; they range from dwarfs and miniature types to upright clumps and towering columns many metres tall. Some icons in the cactus world develop distinctive, almost comical, arm-like branches well above ground. A few highly specialised cacti (*Ariocarpus* species for example) grow partially buried in the soil, and can pull themselves even lower in the soil profile during dry spells.

Epiphytic cacti have a very different appearance to terrestrial cacti. Highly specialised growth modifications enable them to grow on rocks and cliffs as lithophytes, or on mossy tree trunks and branches as epiphytes (both these categories are treated as epiphytes in this book). Epiphytic cacti are mainly found in warm, humid tropical and subtropical forests where a strongly seasonal climate predominates. In such climates periods of intensely heavy rain are separated by long periods without any rain. Epiphytic cacti range from climbers that can cover tree trunks and branches with a mass of scrambling growth (*Hylocereus* species for example) to clumping forms with upright to sprawling leaf-like stems (*Disocactus*), or dangling rope-like stems (*Rhipsalis*).

Right: *Pachycereus weberi* in Mexico

RECOGNISING A CACTUS

To members of the general gardening public a cactus is a prickly plant that grows in desert regions. Generalisations such as this are misleading and it is not surprising that many people apply the term cactus wrongly to a range of succulent plants. A succulent is a plant with the ability to store water internally enabling it to survive periods of seasonal aridity and drought. **It must be emphasised that all cacti are succulents, but not all succulents are cacti.** Often some of the larger or prickly succulents, such as species of *Agave, Aloe* and *Yucca*, are wrongly described as cacti. In the same way some prickly euphorbias are commonly mistaken for cacti.

Cacti then are succulents, and a succulent is a plant with the ability to store water internally in its roots, stems or leaves. There are thousands of species of succulents distributed over a range of plant families. Succulents, including cacti, originate in regions of low rainfall or irregular rainfall, or in climates with long dry spells between rainfall events. Some succulents store water in thick fleshy leaves (leaf succulents) others in swollen stems (stem succulents). Most cacti are stem succulents, although the highly modified photosynthetic stems in some epiphytic cacti (known as cladodes or phylloclades) make it difficult to recognise them as such.

The most significant feature that defines a cactus is the presence of *areoles*. These structures, which are not found in any other group of plants (other succulents included), are specialised buds that appear as small bumps, pads or cushion-like structures on the cactus stem. Areoles are apparently highly modified and much condensed branches or shoots that have evolved as an adaptation to cope with dry habitats. Clusters of spines sprout from the areoles; sometimes these spines are vestigial and resemble hairs or bristles. Roots, branches and flowers can also arise from the areoles.

Spines, which actually represent vestigial leaves, are also a significant feature of cacti. They provide a means of defence for the plant and, despite their small bulk, can also shade the areole and trap a layer of air around it, thus helping to reduce water loss. Spines vary in physical features between various cacti and these characters can sometimes serve as a useful means of distinguishing groups within the family. Some spines are hooked, others straight, some have cross bands, some taper from a broad base, others are thin like needles, while some nasty ones have a supplementary armament of barbs. More than one type of spine can be produced

Right: Mixed cacti and other succulents.

ESPOSTOOPSIS
DYBOWSKI.

from an areole. Often the main central spine(s) is flanked by a series of radiating spines that can be of a different size, shape and colour. In one group of cacti, the *Opuntia* alliance (subfamily Opuntioideae), clumps of detachable hair-like bristles known as glochids arise in the areoles with or without accompanying spines.

Additional growth features found in cacti include widely spreading but shallow root systems that are efficient at gathering water from a range of sources; flowers with numerous sepals, petals and stamens; and smooth, bristly or spiny berry-like fruit that can be dry or have moist flesh, and containing small scattered seeds.

Paul Forster

The spines, dense areole wool and flower buds of *Echinocactus grusonii*

Paul Forster

Ferocactus cylindraceus, flowers and spines

CACTUS NAMES

All plants, including cacti, are classified by a binomial system of nomenclature. Thus the generic name (genus is singular, genera is plural), for example *Opuntia* or *Mammillaria*, when combined with a species epithet such as *microdasys* or *elongata*, makes up the specific binomial name; thus the scientific (or botanical) name *Opuntia microdasys* and *Mammillaria elongata*.

There is much speculation and confusion about the scientific names applied to cacti. Often a species of cactus can have several botanical names. Some of these are incorrect (synonyms) because they do not meet the requirements of the botanical code of nomenclature. Some are synonyms because they are not distinct and fall within the range of variation of another species. Additionally different names may be applied in some countries, regions or states for the same species, and different points of view between scientists researching cacti are quite common. These factors all result in confusion for the hobbyist and amateur grower. Scientific studies also result in name changes, a major bugbear of growers. Modern molecular studies that are shedding light on ancestral relationships will hopefully resolve many of these nomenclatural issues. For consistency with cactus names in this book I have followed the classification of Edward F. Anderson in his comprehensive book *The Cactus Family* published in 2001 by Timber Press. He in turn follows the classification of the International Cactus Systematics Group, which adjusts taxonomy and nomenclature as new research is published. With the aid of fellow botanist and succulent guru Paul Forster, I have also been able to keep abreast of recently published studies, such as the reinstatement of *Trichocereus* as distinct from *Echinopsis*.

WHY GROW CACTI?

Why indeed grow cacti? A good question since so many of these intriguing plants are ferociously armed with incredibly sharp spines. A useful comparison might be found in the much-loved garden rose, since these plants, with their array of stout thorns, must also be handled with care. Roses of course are valued for their variety of lovely flowers that are often exquisitely fragrant. In a similar way, cactus enthusiasts find much of interest and beauty in the highly adapted plants they cherish. Unique growth features, stem and spine colours, decorative spine patterns and surprisingly beautiful (often spectacular) flowers (sometimes also fragrant) provide incentives to take up growing cacti as an enthralling hobby.

Growth Habits: Cacti offer a tremendous diversity of shape, colour and form. Numerous low growing types are available, ranging from partly subterranean novelties to solitary globes, small cylinders and clumpers that form spreading patches and mounds. Large cacti add to the diversity, some appearing to erupt from the ground, others forming massive tree-like structures. Many of the larger-growers have distinct sculptural features that can provide an eye-catching focal point in the garden. Some cacti have thick fleshy taproots or tuberous roots to cope with very dry situations, others have a spreading fibrous root system that can tap the water and nutrients from a wide area. As an example a single root of a large *Ferocactus pringlei* was estimated to extend about 12m through the ground.

Attractive display of the golden-flowered form of *Trichocereus huascha*

Spine Features: Cactus spines add greatly to the beauty of the plant. They embrace a tremendous range of variation in shape, size, ornamentation and arrangement. Spines can add greatly to the appeal of a cactus, especially when a mixed collection is on display. Smooth spineless cacti provide a stark contrast to the spiny types. Some species have drab spines, others are starkly white and certain species have colourful spines, these especially noticeable on growing stem tips. Spine colours can also change with the degree of exposure to the sun and with growth phases during the year. The spines of some *Echinocereus* and *Ferocactus* species for example take on attractive colours (often shades of red) when growing actively in summer.

Cactus Flowers: Many cacti are grown for the beauty of their flowers. Some have small flowers but make up for lack of size with vibrant colours and incredible displays; others produce amazingly flamboyant flowers that rival the beauty of exotic orchids. The majority of cacti flower during the day (termed diurnal flowering) but a significant number have fragrant flowers that open in the evening and at night (nocturnal flowering) to attract specific pollinators such as large moths and bats. Some cactus flowers last just a few hours, others open for several days; some species produce flowers sporadically over many months, whereas others are noted for their massed floral displays. Many cactus flowers, especially those that are tubular towards the base, contain nectar. This sugary exudate attracts nectar-feeding birds such hummingbirds and spinebills, as well as a range of insects, particularly bees, butterflies and hoverflies.

Other Features: A small collection of cacti grown in dedicated area will add a great deal of interest to any garden, displaying a changing range of form, colour, spination and floral features over the seasons. An array of cacti can look especially appealing in a well-lit courtyard where the plants and nocturnal flowers provide an unusual display. From a practical viewpoint, cacti are very good at handling dryness, an important contribution to gardens in times of severe drought, water restrictions and climate change. Small cacti don't mix well with other garden plants and are easily lost, but large growing cacti can provide a dramatic focal point. Cacti also look particularly appealing when grown with rocks, and specialised rockeries are an excellent means of displaying cacti to effect. Cacti are also excellent in containers, needing little maintenance and being forgiving of neglect. Some cacti can also be used successfully for indoor decoration.

Paul Forster

Colourful *Ferocactus* spines

Paul Forster

Hooked spines on *Ferocactus*

Tony Wood

Rebutia steinbachii subsp. *tiraquensis*

Epiphyllum 'Star of Persia'

Tony Wood

Thelocactus bicolor subsp. *schwarzii*

Hatiora rosea

CHOOSING WHICH CACTI TO GROW

Joining a society that specialises in cacti and succulents is a great way to learn about these plants. Societies occur in many states with meetings held at regular intervals throughout the year at which plants are displayed and discussed. Many societies have libraries of specialist magazines and books available for members to borrow, and often there is a monthly talk by a local grower or expert in a particular field. Also there is an annual show put on by members of the society, with associated sales tables for the purchase of plants. Cacti can also be purchased from specialist nurseries, other growers, garden centres and sometimes even chain stores.

Whereas new chums tend to tend to try any species available, experienced growers realise only too well the folly of trying to grow a wide range of cacti that have different growth habits and cultural requirements in the one collection. Hobbyists often tend to specialise in a few groups such as the genus *Mammillaria*, which seems to have a special appeal for growers. Small-growing cacti are especially favoured because of the minimal room they occupy. By contrast the larger-growing cacti can only be held in a container for so long before they must be planted out. These cacti, which can be grown in a specialised part of the garden, are excellent in drier inland areas and semi-arid regions where the local soils and prevailing conditions are ideal for their cultivation.

Tony Wood

Rebutia steinbachii (the variant previously known as *Sulcorebutia krahnii*)

Tony Wood

Stenocactus crispatus

Monstrose growth on the stem of *Cereus hildmannianus*

Ron Tunstall

Grafted crest of *Cleistocactus winteri*

Ron Tunstall

Grafted *Echinopsis chamaecereus* 'Aureus'

Grafted monstrose form, *Astrophytum ornatum*

ABNORMAL GROWTH FORMS

Certain cacti are predisposed to producing abnormal growth features, such as crests, monstrosities and variegations. Unusual growths of these types can often be separated successfully from the parent and grown as a novelty. Stem cuttings and grafting are the usual methods for propagating such plants. Oddities like the abnormal forms mentioned below are of special interest to ardent collectors and many of these novelties have become well established in cultivation.

- ***Crests*** (also known as *cristate* forms and *fasciations*) originate when the growth apex proliferates to form a series of growing points, the final result being a series of flattish fan-like growths that can be straight or wavy. Crests need careful watering to avoid water pooling in the deep folds. Crests can flower, sometimes more prolifically than a normal plant. Crests can also revert back to normal growth.
- ***Monstrose*** growths are not as organised as a crest because the growing points extend in many directions at once, resulting in disorganised, twisted or knobbly structures. Monstrose structures often emerge as side growths on some columnar cacti or can terminate the stem.
- ***Variegations*** are the result of incomplete chlorophyll development in parts of the leaf, usually resulting in white or yellow patches, bands or zones that complement the normal green areas. A good example in Cactaceae is the variegated form of *Opuntia monacantha* known as 'Joseph's Coat'. Variegations in cacti can also embrace whole plants that completely lack chlorophyll resulting in white, cream or yellow plants (*Echinopsis chamaecereus* 'Aureus' for example). Sometimes the chlorophyll loss is masked by the development of anthocyanin pigments resulting in distinctive red- or purple-coloured growths. The classic example here is *Gymnocalycium mihanovichii* which is available in a range of remarkable colour variants, including reds and purples, all propagated by grafting.

EASY CACTI TO START WITH

Astrophytum capricorne Growing to about 20cm tall, this species has long, thin, often twisted spines along prominent ribs. Bright yellow flowers with a red central ring open widely on warm spring days.

Astrophytum myriostigma An unusual, nearly spineless, cactus that is valued for its ribbed globe-like growths that are heavily adorned with scale-like tufts of short silvery-white hairs. Red-throated yellow flowers are produced from the top of the stem in spring.

Cereus hildmannianus Often grown as a feature plant in gardens, this tree-like cactus forms clumps of upright blue-green stems 3–5m tall. Nocturnal fragrant white flowers 15–20cm across open in summer and autumn.

Cleistocactus ritteri This clumping species, which has bright green stems to about 1m tall, tolerates light to moderate frost. Unusual green to light yellow tubular flowers appear at intervals in spring and summer.

Cleistocactus samaipatanus A clumping species with several yellowish-spined stems to about 1m tall. Attractive displays of bright red flowers are produced at intervals in spring and summer.

Cleistocactus strausii A fast-growing species with column-like stems to 1m or more tall, each stem covered densely with thin white spines. Unusual dark red tubular flowers appear in spring and summer. Frost can damage small plants or stem tips.

Cleistocactus winteri With its sprawling yellow-spined stems, this species makes an excellent ground cover or basket plant. It tolerates light to moderate frosts and produces attractive pinkish orange flowers at intervals in spring and summer.

Disocactus flagelliformis Commonly known as the Rat's-tail Cactus, this frost-hardy species is ideal in a hanging container. Its dangling cylindrical stems, covered with masses of pale spines, produce arresting displays of bright pink flowers in spring.

Echinocactus grusonii The popular Golden Ball cactus, often grown as a feature plant in gardens, also does well in a container. Best in full sun, it tolerates light to moderate frost.

Echinocereus adustus Neat grower with attractive spines and lovely pink to purple flowers. Best in a pot. Tolerates frost.

Echinocereus pentalophus Erect to spreading finger-like stems armed with long spines. Startling, large colourful flowers appear in spring sometimes in stunning displays. Grow in a shallow pot or hanging basket.

Golden Ball cacti at Bevan's Cactus Gardens, Lightning Ridge, New South Wales.

Attractive display of the scented flowers of *Trichocereus spachianus*

Clump of *Parodia leninghausii*

Echinopsis chamaecereus The ideal cactus for the beginner. Forms compact to spreading clumps with smallish growths and relatively large showy orange-red flowers. Best in a pot. Takes some frost.

Echinopsis cinnabarina Excellent potplant with a single flattish stem and showy blood-red flowers. Part shade or filtered light. Tolerates some frost.

Echinopsis famatimensis Valued for its neatly ribbed stems and lovely yellow to orange flowers. Best in a pot. Tolerates light frost.

***Echinopsis* hybrids** Clumping plants that are easy to grow. Valued for their displays of large colourful (but short-lived) flowers. Several colour forms are available.

Echinopsis oxygona Tolerant of much neglect, this frost hardy species can be grown in a pot or the garden. Dark green stems with rows of sharp spines. Large pink or white flowers last a day with several batches over summer.

***'Epiphyllum'* hybrids** Easily grown clumpers with flamboyant flowers. Excellent in a hanging pot or basket. Wide range of colours available. Shade or filtered light and no frost.

Gymnocalycium mihanovichii A popular species with a compact growth habit and white to greenish flowers. Best in a pot. Will tolerate light frost. Many colourful mutant cultivars are available as grafted plats.

Gymnocalycium schickendantzii A single-stemmed species with a globose habit and white to reddish flowers that last over several days. Best in a pot. Tolerates some frost.

Hatiora salicornioides Commonly called the Drunkard's Dream because of the bottle-shaped sections of stem. Tolerates a wide range of conditions and neglect. Ideal in a hanging container. Small orange flowers.

Lepismium houlettianum Attractive wavy stems in a large pendulous clump. Small white flowers. Best in a basket. Needs shade or filtered light and no frost.

Mammillaria bombycina Small clumper which has compact growths covered with spines and white wool. Pink flowers encircle the tops of the stems. Tolerates light frost.

Mammillaria compressa Wonderful clumping cactus that eventually forms a mound of pricky stems. Grow in the garden or a large shallow pot. Tolerates light frost.

Mammillaria hahniana Clumper with spines and white bristles. Small pink flowers encircle the stem tops.

Mammillaria longimamma An excellent potplant with neat growth and yellow flowers that last several days. Tolerates slight frost.

Oreocereus celsianus Slow-growing clumper that can be grown in a large pot or as a garden plant. Unusual flowers.

Oreocereus doelzianus Clumping species that forms a shrubby clump (sometimes straggly). In the best form, which is known as var. *sericatus*, the stems are completely covered by fluffy white hairs.

Parodia horstii Sun-lover that flowers several times a year. Solitary or clumping with orange to reddish or purple flowers. Tolerates light frost.

Parodia leninghausii Popular and adaptable species with plump cylindrical stems covered with soft yellow spines. Pot or garden plant. Tolerates light frost if dry.

Parodia magnifica Clumper with large globe-like stems and innocuous spines. Wonderful displays of yellow flowers at the top of mature growths.

Peniocereus serpentinus Tall cactus that can be trained to grow through a shrub. Delightfully scented large spidery flowers produced on spring–autumn nights.

Rebutia steinbachii Fast-growing clumper that forms a dense mound of neat stems. Massed displays of flowers in a range of colours.

Rhipsalis cereuscula Unusual growth habit. Hanging stems with clustered growths and small white flowers. Easily grown and tolerant of a wide range of conditions.

Stenocactus crispatus Compact grower with prominent wavy ribs and purple flowers. Pot or garden. Will tolerate light frost.

Thelocactus bicolor Popular but spiny species with impressive flowers. Best in a pot. Tolerates some frost.

Trichocereus huascha An easily grown frost hardy clumper with thickish growths and large colourful flowers that last two or three days. Red and yellow-flowered forms are available. Large plants produce impressive floral displays.

Trichocereus pachanoi Suitable for a large pot or as a garden plant. Forms a tall clump of nearly spineless stems that produce large white nocturnal flowers. Tolerates light to moderate frost.

Trichocereus spachianus A hardy species that will grow in a range of positions in well-drained soil. Easy to grow and frost hardy, it clumps with slender columnar stems to about 1.5m tall. Lovely white flowers open in the evening and next day.

WEEDY CACTI

Currently more than 40 species of Cactaceae are listed as naturalised weeds in Australia. Easily the worst are species of the subfamily Opuntioideae, especially *Opuntia* (about 20 species naturalised) and to a lesser extent *Cylindropuntia* (nine species) and *Austrocylindropuntia* (two species). Species of *Opuntia* (Prickly Pears) were introduced into Australia in the 1830s and quickly became popular potplants for their unusual growth features, colourful flowers and fruit. They also needed minimum care, propagated without difficulty and were soon planted in gardens and as living fences to keep stock out, and as fodder. Before long the Prickly Pears had 'jumped the fence' and by the 1870s the spread was such that some areas in Queensland and New South Wales had become blocked by a mass of prickly impenetrable growth. By the early 1900s the pest covered over 90 000 square miles and its spread was estimated at about one million acres a year. Control measure such as spraying and burning were ineffective and biological controls were sought. Four species of Cochineal insects were introduced with some success but proved to be relatively specific as to which species they attacked. Eventually in the mid-1920s a tunnelling caterpillar from Argentina became the subject of a detailed breeding and release program. The distribution and feeding activities of this caterpillar, the larvae of the Cactus Moth *Cactoblastis cactorum,* was so effective that by 1932 vast tracts of infested land had been cleared of Prickly Pear. Not all species were affected equally by the moth larvae, and populations of several species of Prickly Pear and other Opuntioids still occur today, not only in inland areas but also near-coastal regions. It must be pointed out that most or all *Opuntia* species are declared noxious weeds in Queensland, New South Wales, South Australia and northern parts of Western Australia; *Opuntia robusta* and *O. vulgaris* are declared in Victoria. Currently there is a move to have them all banned from cultivation nationwide. Some cactus societies also ban Opuntioid cacti from display in shows.

Other species of cacti have become naturalised in Australia but not to the extent of Opuntioid cacti. Three species of *Harrisia* (*H. martinii*, *H. regelii* and *H. tortuosa*) are widely distributed in inland areas of Queensland and New South Wales. These cacti form clumps of tangled prickly stems that can sprawl on the ground, rooting as they grow, or climb into bushes and trees, eventually forming impenetrable thickets. They have tuber-like storage roots that develop underground and can reshoot if the top growth is killed. The soft ripe fruit are eaten by birds which spread the seeds. The Dragon Fruit (*Hylocereus undatus*), so popular for its large edible fruit, is also an occasional garden escape in Queensland

Cereus hildmannianus and *Stapelia gigantea* naturalised at Lightning Ridge

Naturalised *Opuntia*

Opuntia pads infested with a Cochineal insect

Opuntia plant killed by *Cactoblastis* grubs

and New South Wales and the climbing cactus *Pereskia aculeata* is well established as a pest in both states. *Cereus hildmannianus*, the soft fruit of which is eaten by birds and the seeds distributed in their droppings, is also spreading in both states. Seedlings commonly germinate within clumps of shrubs, the mature plants eventually emerging above the canopy. The night flowerer, *Peniocereus serpentinus,* is naturalised in Queensland.

If at all doubtful as to the suitability of a cactus for your garden or collection consult the local council as they usually maintain a list of plants that are considered to be problematical in their area.

HOUSING CACTI

A small collection of cacti can be successfully grown on a sunny verandah or in a modified indoor area, but plant collections have a habit of expanding. For optimum growth, especially in areas with an adverse climate, larger collections must be housed in some way.

Greenhouses and Glasshouses: In temperate regions the shelter and warmth provided by a greenhouse (clad with polythene, rigid plastic or polycarbonate materials) or glasshouse (clad with glass) will enable a greater range of species to be grown. If winter heating is available then the range will be further increased. Cacti grown in a structure of this type will benefit from stabilising effects on temperature as well as protection from winter cold, especially frost. Glass has the best light transmission and does not deteriorate with age, but is heavy and fragile; hailstorms can have devastating effects. Rigid plastics are light, easier to handle and less fragile than glass; however, they can deteriorate with age, especially if cheap grades are used. Only white or clear sheets provide suitable light for cacti growth. The structure should be sited where it receives maximum winter sun as excessive winter shading can be detrimental. Over much of mainland Australia, the amount of light received is largely independent of its orientation (north-south or east-west).

- ***Ventilation:*** Adequate ventilation is of major importance by providing fresh air and cooling the atmosphere on hot days. Ventilators should be situated near the base of walls and in the roof so that an upward flow of air is achieved. Automatic systems are available for roof vents and wall-mounted louvre systems. Small fans help to distribute air evenly around the structure.
- ***Shading:*** Supplementary shading is necessary over summer to avoid sunburn and excessive bleaching of the plants. Shadecloth supported on a frame

20–30cm above the glass effectively counteracts the deleterious effects of too much summer sun. Shadecloth or light-reflective cloth supported within the greenhouse can also be effective.

- ***Humidification:*** Epiphytic cacti appreciate a congenial humid atmosphere that builds up in a greenhouse or glasshouse with time. Humidity is enhanced by watering and using mist sprays and humidifiers.

Shadehouses and Bushhouses: A solid roofed structure of this type (with shadecloth around the sides) will reduce plant damage caused by heavy rainfall and drips and provide some shelter for cacti while still giving excellent aeration. It also reduces the impact of winter rain, which can be devastating on dormant plants and provides some protection from light frosts (but minimal protection from heavy frost). Chilling and draught protection can also be gained by having a solid wall along the side that is exposed to cold winds.

Below: Part of the large collection at Cactus County, Strathmerton, Victoria.

Part of the author's collection of epiphytic cacti.

Paul Forster

Display garden in greenhouse at Orana Cactus World, Gilgandra, New South Wales.

PESTS, DISEASES AND MALADIES OF CACTI

MEALY BUGS

These are probably the commonest, most persistent and most annoying pest that attacks cacti. Growing 1–3mm long, the adults have a plump, soft body that is covered with white powder and waxy threads. A number of species are known, the females producing either live young or numerous eggs crowded in white waxy or powdery sacs. Thankfully the females die after egg laying, but unfortunately they are replaced by tiny yellow crawlers that hatch from the eggs in a few days and can disperse to new feeding sites. The crawlers mature in six to eight weeks and several life cycles occur in a year. Mealy bugs, especially the Long-tailed Mealy Bug, relish the warm humid conditions of greenhouses and glasshouses. These pests are visible as white blobs and the area where they feed is commonly covered with white powder and littered with waxy threads. They feed by sucking sap, resulting in damage to growth and causing yellow areas that can become infected with sooty mould. They congregate on the sheltered parts of plants such as the junction between offsets, stem axils, under bracts, sheaths and spine clusters. They can even find a home in the potting mix, feeding on cactus roots. Their feeding activities can cause serious plant damage, including bud drop, growth distortion and plant death. Control can be difficult and needs vigilance and persistence. Dabbing with methylated spirits is useful for cleaning up small infestations, but fortnightly spraying with a recommended pesticide is necessary to eliminate persistent outbreaks.

SCALE INSECTS

These insects occur either as isolated individuals or form colonies. They live beneath the shelter of a waxy covering and suck the plant's sap. At intervals they reproduce producing tiny crawlers that can spread to new feeding sites. Several species attack cacti, either persisting as individuals or forming dense patches and spreading colonies. Control is generally by spraying with an oil-based spray such as eco oil or half strength white oil and Maldison. Pyrethrum based sprays can also be useful at the crawling stage. Note that damage from oil-based sprays can occur when used at full strength, and at temperatures above 25°C.

APHIDS OR GREENFLY

A common persistent pest that congregates in colonies and sucks the sap from young buds, resulting in distortion and bud drop. These insects can also transmit

Mealy Bug infestation of cactus roots

Long-tailed mealy bugs on *Aporophyllum* flower

Palm Scale on *Epiphyllum* stem

White Louse Scale on *Epiphyllum* stem

viruses, and their feeding activity is often followed by outbreaks of sooty mould. Control is by using suitable contact sprays, such as Pyrethnum.

SPIDER MITES

These tiny eight-legged animals are among the most persistent and damaging pests of plants. They increase quickly in warm dry conditions and spread rapidly from plant to plant, spinning fine webs beneath which they shelter and feed. They feed by sucking plant sap and in cacti usually congregate on the dry side of a stem and under spine clusters. They can be severe on pectinate-spined cacti such as species of *Echinocereus* and *Thelocactus*. Afflicted tissue appears dry with a yellow blotched appearance. Severe attacks can result in the stems taking on a bronzed appearance or becoming silvery grey-green. These pests, which prefer dry conditions, can be discouraged by misting. Complete control, usually involving the application of suitable sprays (miticides), is generally difficult because spider mites breed quickly and are renowned for developing resistance to chemical sprays. A predator mite is available from biological control firms.

SLUGS AND SNAILS

These pests, which enjoy warm humid conditions, are very destructive of epiphytic cacti but can also cause damage to other types. They especially enjoy soft fleshy growth and also feed on buds, spent flowers and fruit. Control is by baiting with commercial pellets, hand picking at night with the aid of a torch, or drowning in traps containing stale beer. Take care to remove mouldy snail bait pellets, as they can induce Grey Mould and other rots to develop in sensitive plant tissues.

CROWN ROT

This is a condition in cacti whereby the apical part of a stem becomes soft and collapses. This can result in the death of the affected growth or the whole plant may die. Often, however, the affected area becomes sealed off and the disease progresses no further, but leaves an unsightly scar. Such damaged stems may survive but do not grow any more. The causal agent is possibly a species of the fungus genus *Phythophthora*, and the disease often strikes after prolonged periods of showery weather or heavy rain. It can sometimes also appear following heavy fruit set, particularly if the fruit rot while still attached to the plant. Applications of phosphorous acid (not phosphoric) may give some control, or at least stop development of the infection.

SOOTY MOULD

This is an unsightly blackish stain caused by a fungus that grows on the waste products exuded from colonies of sucking pests, such as aphids and mealy bugs. Eliminating the sucking pest is usually sufficient to control the mould which disappears with time. Certain cacti, including species of *Ferocactus* and *Thelocactus*, produce sugary exudates from the areoles which can lead to the unsightly development of Sooty Mould.

GREY MOULD OR BOTRYTIS ROT

This fungus develops on damaged leaf tissue or decaying plant parts such as spent flowers or rotting fruit. It can also develop on decaying pellets used to control slugs and snails. The disease forms a fuzzy grey covering on the affected part which eventually collapses and decays. This fungus favours warm humid conditions (such as in a greenhouse) and can spread rapidly from infected areas into healthy plant tissue. Control is by hygiene (removing spent plant parts and snail baits before decay), improving ventilation, and spraying with suitable fungicides.

POOR DRAINAGE AND OVERWATERING

Poor soil drainage is the number one killer of cultivated cactus plants. The root system dies first, followed by death of the plant. Plant collapses and rotting can be rapid and dramatic. Often the plant becomes yellow or bleached before it dies. Affected plants also lack a healthy sheen and look like they are not thriving. A clue to the problem is that they are unstable in the pot indicating that anchorage is poor due to root death. The overwatering of cactus plants and growing them in unsuitable potting mix also produces similar results. Deaths in garden-grown cactus plants, which often follow periods of heavy rain, are more prominent in wet years.

MALINGERERS

Unthrifty plants can result from a range of conditions including overwatering, underwatering, poor nutrition and lack of ventilation. Affected plants do not thrive, look unthrifty and are often subject to persistent attacks by pests such as scale and mealy bugs.

ETIOLATION

Cactus plants require bright light for optimum growth. Plants grown in too much shade or those grown as indoor plants often suffer from abnormal growth that

Cutting taken from a plant with stem rot, cut surface treated with powdered sulphur

Death of cactus stem tip caused by crown rot

Epiphyllum severely damaged by heavy frost

Ferocactus stem malformation caused by crown rot

appears as if stretched or drawn out. Etiolated plants grown indoors usually lean to the nearest light source. Etiolated growth is usually pale green or yellowish and the distance between areoles appears abnormal for the species. Damage caused by etiolation is permanent but the affected plant will respond positively if moved into brighter light (beware of sunburn though).

STEM SPLITS

Splits in cactus plants are usually associated with too much water uptake. Cacti are very efficient at taking up water but heavy rainfall or inappropriate watering can result in excess water uptake by the plant. Splitting seems to be worst in summer when the plants are in active growth. It can also be exacerbated by heavy spring rain following soon after fertiliser or manure application. Splits persist on the plant and are usually isolated by scar tissue but can lead to the entry of fungal rots.

SUNBURN

It is surprising to associate cacti with sunburn; however, it is not an infrequent occurrence. Sun-damaged areas initially show up as yellow patches that become necrotic and can spread as a rot or persist as ugly brown scars. Sunburn is most commonly seen after cactus plants have been moved suddenly from a shady or sheltered site (such as a verandah or greenhouse) into the sun. This damage can be avoided by moving plants early in the season before the sun is too hot or hardening off plants by gradually increasing their exposure to sun over a couple of weeks. Sun damage may occasionally occur when water is present on the surface of a plant during the heat of a summer's day. Water-induced sun damage results in scarring around the crown of the cactus plant.

FROST DAMAGE

Frost damage results in necrotic areas and unsightly brown scars similar to sunburn. It can also cause stem cracking and the death of growing points, resulting in growth malformation and rotting leading to plant death. The death of stem tips is not infrequent in some columnar cacti, such as *Cleistocactus strausii*. Seedling cacti are also much more susceptible to frost than mature plants. In epiphytic cacti, frost-damaged stem tips lead to rotting that can spread through a single growth or even the whole plant.

Cacti originating in the tropical lowlands are very easily killed by frost. Similarly, cacti from coastal districts have limited frost tolerance and can be damaged or killed even by a light frost. By contrast, cacti from high altitudes in the mountains and desert areas exposed to cold winters, are much more tolerant of cold and frost. The impact of frost on cacti is, however, much worse if the soil is wet following heavy rain in late autumn or winter. Damage is also worse if the first frosts of the season are heavy because a succession of early light frosts hardens plants allowing them to acclimatise before the arrival of severe frost. Hardening off plants in autumn, by reducing or stopping watering, is important for their survival over winter.

PROPAGATING CACTI

Cacti can be propagated from seed (known as sexual propagation) or by using vegetative techniques (asexual propagation). Vegetative propagation produces larger cactus plants more quickly than by seed, but fewer plants can be produced. Cacti propagated by vegetative means will be identical to the parent plant, whereas those grown from seed may vary in a range of features, especially spination and flower colour. Grafting, which is also a vegetative technique, can also play an important role in cactus propagation.

Vegetative Propagation

Because most vegetative techniques of propagation are relatively straightforward, they are often used by hobbyists to increase numbers. Selected forms or cultivars must be propagated vegetatively if they are to retain their unique characteristics. The best time to propagate cacti is during spring and early summer when they establish quickly, not in winter when the plants are dormant. Two methods are available.

Offsets: Many cacti grow in clumps and spread by the formation of side growths or offsets. These growths are prominent at the base of a mature plant or on the margins of a clump. Offsets are easily separated from the clump and can be grown as individual plants. Those offsets that have their own roots will establish quickly once separated, but leafless offsets need to be treated as a cutting and dried out for a week or two before planting. Damaged areas should be sealed with lime or sulphur powder to reduce the incidence of rotting.

Stem Cuttings: This is a rather drastic technique that involves slicing transversely across a stem and using the top section as a cutting. It is used for terrestrial cacti that have cylindrical stems and also columnar types. It is also the main method for propagating epiphytic cacti. Cutting length varies (minimum 10–15cm long) but as a general guide the larger the cactus the larger the cutting that is taken (within reason). The area of the basal cut must be allowed to dry and form a seal for a couple of weeks before the cutting is planted, otherwise rotting may occur. Cut areas can also be sealed with lime or sulphur powder to reduce the incidence of rotting. When the base is well sealed, the cutting can be potted or planted directly in the ground. A simple technique for handling large prickly stem cuttings is to attach two bamboo stakes firmly to the cutting via strong twine or plastic coated garden wire. These stakes, which allow the cutting to be manouevered easily, are pushed into the ground beside the cutting at planting time to provide support until roots form. Cuttings are best planted shallowly, with the base at or just below soil level.

Cactus stem cuttings

Seed Propagation

Raising cacti from seed is the best method for building up numbers and also avoids the problems associated with virus diseases since these are mostly not transmitted through the seed. Seedlings generally resemble the parent, but can differ, especially if hybridisation has occurred.

Sowing Time: Seeds are best sown early in the growing season (early spring) when there is maximum time for germination and early growth. For cacti that shed their seeds in winter it is best to store the seed and sow in spring.

Collecting Seed: Remove fruit when ripe (ripe fruit are generally soft and highly coloured), slice open and squeeze out the flesh and seeds onto paper towel. Dry quickly and remove the seeds. Sow seeds immediately or air dry them and store until needed.

Sowing Technique: Pots or trays of a freely draining mix are used for seed propagation. A suitable mix can be made using equal parts washed sand and good quality potting mix. Sieve the mix through a 1mm or 2mm sieve, discarding the larger particles. Fill the pot or tray close to the top, pat down gently and sow the seeds sparsely over the soil surface. Some growers sterilise the mix in a microwave before sowing. Remember to label the pots to avoid confusion. Avoid overcrowding seed if possible. Cover the seeds with a thin layer of fine sand. Water the newly sown seeds by standing the pot or tray in shallow water until the top of the potting mix becomes moist. Drain the pot and cover with a sheet of glass or place in a plastic bag (not freezer bag). Some terrestrial cacti, such as species of *Lophophora*, can be raised in enclosed plastic containers with aeration holes in the lid.

Keep the pots in a warm, brightly lit area (no direct sun). Some growers find a bottom heat unit effective for seed germination. Check the pots regularly, keeping the mix moist (by misting) but not too wet or too dry.

Germination will vary with the species, taking from two weeks to many months (difficult species may take years to appear). When a good strike is apparent the glass cover or plastic bag should be quickly removed. Initially the young plants are watered by regular misting but as they grow they are best watered by standing the pot in shallow water (as for newly sown seeds). Be observant for fungal diseases. Provide bright but diffuse light (not full sun) as the plants grow and gradually decrease watering to harden the plants off. They can be potted separately when large enough to survive on their own.

Epiphytic cacti are propagated in more humid conditions than used for most terrestrial cacti. The freshly dried seeds are either sown on seedling mix in plastic containers with aeration holes in the lid or a whole pot is sealed in a plastic bag (not a freezer bag) and left in a warm place until the seedlings germinate (sometimes taking several months). Often the young plants develop quite fast using these techniques; however, the pots must be observed closely as rots can spread quickly in the humid atmosphere.

Grafting Cacti

Grafting is an important procedure used to aid the cultivation of difficult-to-grow species, as well as novelties including variegated forms, crests and monstrosities. The techniques, which are straightforward and not difficult to master, involve grafting a selected piece of one cactus (the top part of the graft which is termed the ***scion***) onto a rooted section of another cactus (the basal part of the graft which known as the ***rootstock***). Most cactus grafts involve mature plants but even young seedlings only a few weeks old can be successfully grafted. Grafting seedlings requires patience, special skills and good eyesight.

Ron Tunstall

Grafted *Gymnocalycium mihanovichii* orange mutant

Ron Tunstall

Grafted *Gymnocalycium mihanovichii* rose-purple mutant

Advantages of Grafting: Cacti that are slow growing on their own roots or with a weak root system are often grafted to improve vigour. They generally grow more rapidly when grafted and this technique can be used as a method to increase material available for propagation. Removing the top growth from such grafts usually results in a proliferation of offsets which in turn can be removed and grafted or rooted down. Oddball variants of cacti that completely lack chlorophyll must be grafted because they cannot survive on their own roots. Crested forms can sometimes be grown on their own roots but develop much more strongly when grafted. These grafted specimens also add a novel appearance to a collection. Novelty combinations can also be made by grafting epiphytic cacti such as *Schlumbergera* and 'Aporocacti' onto *Opuntia* or *Selenicereus*. Grafting can also be used to save dying or sickly plant if it can be cut back to fresh tissue beyond the point of obvious decay.

Grafting Tools: These include two thin-bladed knives, one very sharp for the final cuts (a scalpel or razor blade can be used for small cacti), tongs for handling the prickly parts, scissors for removing unwanted spines, rubber bands of various sizes, some long, clean cactus thorns and alcohol for sterilising.

Rootstock Type: Columnar cacti, particularly *Trichocereus bridgesii, T. spachianus*, *T. pachanoi* and *Myrtillocactus geometrizans* are commonly used as a rootstock for grafting globular cacti. Short rootstocks mean that the developing grafted plants will appear as if growing on their own roots; longer rootstocks produce an entirely different effect. Long sections of *Nyctocereus serpentinus* and *Selenicereus* can be used for grafting thin-stemmed hanging cacti such as *Disocactus flagelliformis* and other 'Aporocacti'. Opuntias, preferably the less spiny forms, can be used as a rootstock for epiphytes including 'Epiphyllums', *Schlumbergera* and *Hatiora*.

Rootstock Preparation: The rootstocks should be potted and well-established several months before the grafting is to occur. A better grafting match is obtained if the diameter of the rootstock and scion are of a similar diameter or the rootstock is a little larger. The more vigorous and healthier the rootstock the better the results when grafted. Sickly, too-dry or woody rootstocks produce poor results. Small rootstocks can be kept whole until grafting time but large rootstocks suffer shrinkage of the cut surface so it is wise to behead about one month earlier to allow shrinkage to take place. The rootstock is then recut at grafting time by removing a thin slice to expose fresh tissue

Grafting Time: Cacti are best grafted from late spring to mid-summer when the warm weather is conducive to a rapid seal between the cut surfaces.

Grafting Techniques: Strict cleanliness is essential for successful grafting. Wipe all blades with an alcohol-soaked cloth before use. In the commonest form of grafting the rootstock is beheaded with a single flat slicing cut (do not saw the cut). A piece of the plant to be grafted (scion) is taken using a similar cutting technique. The freshly cut edges of both the stock and scion are then bevelled at a steep angle and any hindering spines trimmed back. The two exposed surfaces are then recut by taking a thin slice from each with a very sharp knife. Match the cambium rings closely in each piece (this may mean that the scion is slightly off-centre). A gentle twist removes any air trapped between the two surfaces. The matching of the two cut surfaces must be done quickly to avoid any loss of sap and drying of the exposed tissue. If either cut surface is exposed for any length of time and appears dryish a new thin slice should be removed just before the actual graft is made. The scion is held firmly (but not too tightly) in place by suitably sized rubber bands (two bands at right angles to each other). Some growers use stretchy laboratory film instead of rubber bands. Any sideways movement or slippage of the scion can be prevented by anchoring it with a couple of long cactus spines (*Opuntia* spines are often used). Do not use metal pins.

The scions of thin-stemmed cacti (such as the variegated forms of Peanut Cactus) are best cut on a slant to increase the surface area of contact between the scion and the rootstock. The scion is then laid down on an angle across the rootstock and secured with cactus thorns. Offsets developing close to the base will eventually hide the graft union.

'Epiphyllums' can be successfully grafted into the pads of Opuntias. A pad is cut off at the base leaving a short neck into which a vertical cut 6–8cm deep is made. A scion, with a wedge-shaped basal cut of similar length is inserted into the rootstock and fastened by a cactus spine.

'Aporocactus' can be grafted onto a *Nyctocereus* rootstock using a simple side graft. Matching slanting cuts are made on both the scion and the rootsock which are bound together with wool or laboratory film.The binding material is removed after two weeks or so when the graft has taken.

Schlumbergera and *Hatiora* species and cultivars can be grafted onto *Opuntia* pads using a wedge graft. Either a single sloping cut on the base of the scion or a cut on both sides to form a wedge, allows it to be inserted into the rootstock where a thin wedge of tissue has been removed. The scion is held in place by a cactus spine which is removed after about a week.

Aftercare: The grafted plant should be held in a warm well-ventilated place out of direct sun for 10–14 days after which the rubber bands and spines can be removed. Some growers keep the grafts in high humidity for 3–5 days to help them take, but be careful of rotting (an aquarium or closed polythene box is suitable). Any exposed area around the graft should be kept dry until it callouses over, after which water entry will be effectively avoided. Any offsets that develop on the rootstock should be removed as soon as noticed as they will compete with the graft for energy.

Tony Wood

Acanthocalycium spiniflorum

Echinocereus nivosus

Part Two

GROWING TERRESTRIAL CACTI

Many cacti are easy to grow providing their basic needs are met, whereas some others are much more demanding. In summary the basic needs for the successful cultivation of terrestrial cacti are:

- ***Drainage:*** All cacti need excellent soil drainage, whether grown in a pot or the garden. This point cannot be emphasized enough. Excellent drainage means that any water passes quickly through the soil profile or potting mix, allowing air (oxygen) to be available for root health.
- ***Warmth:*** Most cacti need warmth and cannot handle extreme cold, especially heavy frost. A much greater range of cacti can be grown without shelter in the subtropics and coastal sites than in frosty temperate zones.
- ***Sunshine:*** Most cacti benefit from exposure to sun. Some are happy in full sun, others prefer morning sun or filtered sun.
- ***Air movement:*** Cacti like an open airy position.
- ***Water:*** Despite the fact that cacti are water misers, they need supplementary watering when in active growth from spring to early autumn.
- ***Nutrients:*** Cacti need food like any other plant.
- ***Pests:*** Protection from pests, especially mealy bug and scale, is strongly recommended.

GENERAL REQUIREMENTS

Container or garden: Cacti are commonly grown in pots, although a selection of adaptable species can also be grown in the ground. Most are grown in a pot or some other container because general garden conditions are not always suitable. Some of the larger growing types are suitable as feature plants in a garden, whereas the smaller-growers tend to get lost among other plants. The creation of a special garden dedicated to cacti (against a warm brick wall for example) can solve some of these problems.

pH: Cacti favour slightly acidic soil or potting mix with a pH of between 6 and 6.5. However a range of cacti grow well in soil or potting mix with a slightly alkaline reaction. Where garden soils are more acidic than pH 6, some correction with garden lime may be necessary. Although many cacti grow naturally in limestone areas, it should be noted that the soil in these areas is generally acidic, not alkaline, as is often assumed.

Frost: Frost has a major impact on the selection of species that can be grown in an area (see also page 55). The damaging impact of frost can be avoided or reduced by growing the cacti in a greenhouse, under eaves, or providing temporary winter cover. Some growers protect sensitive cacti in winter by using simple frames constructed from light tubing and polythene sheeting. Bubble wrap can provide a simple and effective frost blanket when wrapped around the top of a valuable plant (it also prevents water collecting and freezing in the sunken tops of Golden Ball cacti).

Sun: Sun damage is not uncommon in cacti, a fact that is not generally appreciated by gardeners. Whereas many cacti need maximum sunlight for optimum growth, there are a number that don't appreciate full summer sun at all, and will only look happy when growing in diffuse light or where they receive sun for only part of the day. In nature many of the smaller cacti gain shelter from shrubs and rocks and they need similar conditions in cultivation.

Watering: Because cacti are renowned for their drought resistance, the watering of cultivated plants causes more anguish to growers than it should. Two points must be made here. More cacti die from overwatering than any other cause. On the other hand no plant can survive without water and there is a limit to the amount of dryness that even a cactus can withstand. Watering is essential for their health while the plants are in growth mode (late spring to early autumn) and they should be kept dry while dormant over winter (small cactus seedlings and some cacti, such as species of *Melocactus*, do not like to dry out completely over winter). Watch the plants and begin watering at the first sign of active growth. Intervals between waterings vary with the weather. Some growers allow the mix to dry out between applications, others do not let the mix dry out completely when the plants are growing actively during the warm weather. In cold weather it is best to stop watering completely. Occasional misting will help to prevent plants shrivelling.

Feeding: Cacti benefit from a balanced feeding regime but are best not overfed. Choose fertilisers low in nitrogen and high in potassium. Feed cacti only in late spring or early summer. Avoid feeding in late summer and autumn, allowing the plants to harden prior to winter.

Weeding: Weeding cacti can be a tricky procedure and it is best to tackle any weeds that appear while they are young. Some of the worst weeds, such as Creeping Oxalis, often germinate very close to the base of the cactus and can be very hard to remove once established. Long-bladed knives or sharpened paint scrapers are useful for cutting into the weeds root system while avoiding the cactus spines. Long-handled tweezers and straight-bladed hemostats are particularly useful for removing weeds that germinate at the base of cactus plants or between offsets in cactus clumps.

Stenocactus coptogonus

Decorative hanging pot of *Schlumbergera* hybrid

Rebutia steinbachii in a decorative pot

Trichocereus spachianus and other succulents in a decorative setting

GROWING CACTI IN CONTAINERS

Most cacti are grown in a container of some type. Containers have many advantages over garden plants not the least being control of the potting mix, feeding and watering. Additionally the containers can be readily moved to avoid frost, heavy rain or hot sun. Dormant cacti can also be moved to a position where they can be kept dry until growth resumes.

Choice of Container

Cacti will grow in a wide range of containers and the type chosen is based mainly on personal choice. Terracotta (preferably use those that are pre-sealed) and glazed concrete pots are commonly used, but plastic pots and tubs can be just as successful. Containers with straight sides are easier to remove plants from at repotting time than those with curved sides. Shallow containers dry out more quickly then deeper ones and require more regular watering. Conversely, deep containers have a proportionately smaller reservoir of moist to wet soil at the base and hence reduce the chance of root rot. Deep containers are essential for cacti that have tuberous roots. Whatever the container, make sure there are enough holes in the base to ensure good drainage.

Potting Mixes

A good cactus mix must drain quickly and be very porous, providing good aeration soon after watering. In the 1950s cactus growers in Melbourne successfully used mixes containing soil and well-rotted manure (for example one-third each of good garden loam, cow manure or sheep manure (or well-rotted leaf mould) and coarse river sand). The soil used was either good quality sandy loam from areas near the coast, or red loam from the mountains. For cacti with fleshy tuberous roots a mix of one part coarse river sand and one part leaf mould was used.

Mammillaria elongata removed from pot to show strong root growth in a perfect potting mix

Modern commercial potting mixes are available for the growth of cacti but these mixes are very high in organic matter and many growers still prefer to concoct their own mix. A simple mix can be made by adding equal parts coarse river sand or gravel to the commercial potting mix (some growers use two-thirds coarse sand and one-third potting mix). The addition of coarse river gravel ensures the continuation of good drainage when the organic material in the mix breaks down with age. However, river sand or gravel is heavy and sinks to the bottom of a pot over time. Perlite, which is much lighter than river sand or gravel, functions in the same way by keeping the mix open and ensuring good drainage and aeration. It, however, tends to float to the surface of a pot with time and can blow away in the wind. Scoria (5–10mm diameter) is also a very useful material to add to a cactus mix. It varies in pH, some samples being quite alkaline. A successful mix can be made from one-third commercial potting mix, one third scoria and one-third coarse river sand. Other materials that can be used for a cactus mix include decomposed granite (select the coarser grades with minimum clay content) and pumice. Growers in Queensland often use a coarse gravelly type of ash (fly ash) as the basis for a successful potting mix.

Commercial potting mixes must be handled with care as they can contain toxic bacteria such as those which cause legionnaire's disease. Always wear a mask and gloves, open the bags carefully so as to avoid the dusty air which vents when the bag is opened, allow to stand for a period before potting, and wash hands, face and equipment thoroughly after use.

Watering

Container-grown cacti should be watered regularly from late spring to early autumn, allowing the potting mix to dry out between waterings. Watering frequency will increase during spells of hot weather and be reduced during cool weather. Sufficient water should be applied to wet the mix, allowing excess to drain through the profile. Watering frequency is reduced in autumn and the plants should be kept dry over winter, resuming watering in spring as the weather warms up. Most growers water in the morning allowing the plants to dry out during the day. Minimise splashing water onto the plants as this can result in damage. Cacti also benefit from light misting during dry periods but not when the plants are in the sun.

Feeding

Blood and bone mixed in with the potting compost will provide nutrients for early growth after potting. Container-grown cacti respond to small doses of fertiliser applied at regular intervals. Avoid fertilisers with high nitrogen content as they produce soft plants that flower poorly. Slow-release fertilisers are particularly effective for container-grown cacti, especially compounds high in potassium and low in nitrogen. Liquid fertilisers with a similar nutrient balance can also be very beneficial. Fertilise with potassium in summer to help initiate flowers.

Repotting

Container-grown cacti need repotting when the pot becomes full of roots and the potting mix is exhausted. Plants in need of repotting often look dull and jaded. Repotting will normally be necessary every one to three years depending on the size of the plant. Repotting is best carried out in spring and early summer, with most of the growing season ahead. Loosen the plant in the pot by squeezing the sides of a plastic pot or tapping the side of a terracotta pot on a hard surface. Hold the plant in position in the new pot with kitchen tongs or a folded or twisted page of newspaper, add the potting mix and firm down around the plant. Tap the pot to settle the soil leaving the soil surface about 1cm below the rim of the pot for watering. Do not water repotted plants for a few days to allow any damaged roots to heal.

General Hints

- Outdoor containers should be supported above the soil surface to prevent the entry through the drainage holes of pests, such as grubs, slaters, earwigs and root diseases.
- Shallow containers dry out more quickly then deeper ones and require more regular watering.
- Deep containers have a proportionately smaller reservoir of moist to wet soil at the base and hence reduce the chance of root rot.
- Avoid damage to the fleshy roots of tuberous cacti as this can lead to rotting. Trim any damaged roots and allow them to dry before repotting.

Indoor Cacti

Perhaps surprisingly, some cacti can be used successfully for indoor decoration. Cacti that are to be grown or displayed indoors must be able to tolerate some neglect, low to moderate levels of light and a dry atmosphere. They are best placed where they receive some light through an archway, window, skylight or doorway, but avoid direct hot sun through glass, especially summer sun.

The extensive root system of this *Trichocereus* was strong enough to break this pot.

GROWING CACTI IN THE GARDEN

Within the Cactaceae are a number of genera that are suitable only for growing in a garden or rockery where sufficient space is available for them to show off their ornamental features and reach maturity. Cacti grown in outdoor gardens often take on a very different appearance to the same species grown in pots. If the climate is suitable, the outdoor conditions, particularly bright light and abundant fresh air, result in healthy plants with natural shape, good colour and evenly distributed, well-developed spines. Additionally cacti grown in the garden often flower more profusely than pot-grown subjects.

Dry Gardens: Areas against the north-facing wall of a house or under extended eaves generally receive less rain than open areas in the garden and may also gain winter warmth and benefit from reduced frost levels. These areas can be used to advantage by creating a 'dry garden' where frost-sensitive or difficult cacti can be grown. Supplementary watering will probably be necessary to maintain plant health during long dry periods.

Cacti in the Arid Landscape: Because of their various adaptations to deserts and semi-desert regions, cacti grow very well as garden plants in inland regions with a semi-arid climate. Frost is again the major limiting factor but if well-drained soil is available an appealing cactus garden can be readily established using adaptable species. Cacti in inland gardens generally grow quite fast, flower freely and develop good appearance, colour and spination.

Soil Type: Well-drained loam or sandy loam is best for growing cacti in the ground. Avoid clay and clay loams where poor drainage limits what can be grown. Cacti grown in sandy soils may require more regular watering than those in heavier soils.

Soil Drainage: Good to excellent drainage is of major importance for the successful cultivation of cacti in the garden. Soil drainage can be improved by raising the level of the beds where the cacti are to be grown. A simple technique is to dig sunken paths around the garden bed and use the removed soil to increase the garden depth. Raised rockeries are also very effective for cacti.

Frost: Frost is a major factor limiting the range of cacti that can be grown in an area (see also page 38). Frost tolerance is difficult to predict (most knowledge is gained from bitter experience) but we can generalise. Some plants that withstand light frosts (0°C to –2°C) will suffer severe damage in a moderate frost (–3°C to –5°C) or be killed in a heavy frost (lower than –6°C). Even hardy cacti can suffer damage from very heavy frost or prolonged periods of frost, especially if they are

Attractive display of the red-flowered form of *Trichocereus huascha*

Echinopsis hybrid 'Greengold' mulched with river stones

in growth mode at the time. The impact of frost on garden-grown cacti can be reduced by planting on slopes where air circulation is unimpeded, planting close to a large rock or against a north-facing wall.

Sun: Garden-grown cacti tend to grow slower than their potted cousins and are mostly tolerant of harsh summer sun, especially after they have adapted to the local garden conditions. Some of the smaller cacti may benefit from partial shelter provided by shrubs, leafy tree canopies, large rocks, or siting them where they only receive morning sun.

Wind: Tall-growing cacti can be damaged by strong winds and may benefit from staking (strong stakes are needed). Strong winds with or soon after heavy rain can result in whole plants, roots and all, being blown out of the ground. Large rocks placed at the base of a tall plant can add some stability. Some wind protection can be gained by planting in the lee of walls, buildings or adjacent to existing shrubs and trees.

Planting Time: Cacti are best planted in the garden in spring as they then have a full spring–summer season to establish. Planting in cold temperate areas is best delayed until the worst of the winter weather is over.

Planting Technique: First dig a hole to the required depth. Remove the plant from the pot (loosen the plant by squeezing the sides of a plastic pot or tapping the side of a terracotta pot on a hard surface). Either handle the plant via the root system or hold the stem with kitchen tongs, or folded or twisted newspaper. Some growers remove the potting soil to avoid any problems arising from disparity with the garden soil. Plant the cactus and fill any gaps with soil. If the soil is very dry water immediately after planting, otherwise allow the plant to settle for a week or so before watering.

Watering: Watering is not a major activity required for garden-grown cacti, as most benefit from natural rainfall. However, some watering may be need in periods of drought or prolonged dry summers. Water the plants during the morning or evening, but avoid the heat of the day. Minimise splashing the plants as this can lead to scarring or rotting.

Feeding: Garden-grown cacti benefit from a balanced feeding regime but are best not overfed. Organic fertilisers, such as blood and bone, and aged animal manures (definitely not fresh) release a steady supply of nutrients for growth and are also beneficial to the health of the soil. Pelleted manures are also useful. Inorganic fertilisers (choose those with a balanced mix of nutrients that are not too high in nitrogen) are readily soluble and supply nutrients quickly to the plants, but should be used sparingly. Feed cacti only in late spring or early summer, preferably just before rain. Avoid feeding in late summer and autumn, allowing the plants to harden prior to winter.

Mulching: Mulching cacti with river stones or coarse gravel will allow the base of the plants to dry out quicker after watering or rain. Using light coloured material will also reflect light and add greatly to the appearance of the pot or garden. Organic mulches, such as bark, are best avoided for cacti.

Parodia magnifica grown among rocks and river pebbles

Acanthocalycium klimpelianum

TERRESTRIAL CACTI TO GROW

ACANTHOCALYCIUM

A genus of three species of globe-like to cylindrical solitary cacti from Argentina. The stems are strongly ribbed and have clumps of needle-like spines. Funnel-shaped flowers arising near the top of a stem open during the day. Ideal for a pot, these cacti need good drainage, unimpeded air movement and dry winter rest. Some will tolerate cold. Increase by seed.

Acanthocalycium klimpelianum

An easily grown species that will tolerate light to moderate frost. The deeply ribbed stem can grow to about 10cm across. White flowers (occasionally pink) about 4cm across open widely at intervals over summer.

Acanthocalycium spiniflorum

Usually solitary, this species has spiny globe-like stems that elongate to cylinders up to 50cm long and 15cm wide. White, pink or violet flowers 5–7cm across open in late spring and summer. This species will tolerate light to moderate frost (photo page 45).

ACHARAGMA

This genus consists of two small cacti from northern Mexico. Usually solitary, but sometimes forming small clumps, these cacti are densely spiny. Usually grown in a small pot, they need excellent drainage, good ventilation and dry winter rest. Increase by seed or division.

Acharagma roseana

An interesting cactus which has short cylindrical stems covered with yellow spines. Unusual pink to reddish or orange flowers with darker midribs are produced from near the stem apex in spring. This species, which has a taproot and needs careful watering at all times, will tolerate light frost.

Paul Forster

Ariocarpus fissuratus

Tony Wood

Acharagma roseana

Ariocarpus retusus

ARIOCARPUS

Unique within the cactus family, these rugged, spineless plants have large fleshy turnip-like taproots and hard leaf-like tubercles arranged like a starfish. Well camouflaged in their surroundings, many species remain buried below ground with only the tubercles showing. In all there are six species, most from Mexico, one also in Texas. Being of very slow growth, these unusual cacti are often grafted to improve the growth rate. They need bright light, good drainage, good ventilation and dry winter rest. Some growers use alkaline mix for these cacti. Avoid water lying on the plant. Increase from seed.

Ariocarpus fissuratus Star Rock Cactus

The tubercles of this species are adorned with numerous crevices and fissures. It is native to Texas and Mexico where it grows on limestone hills and ridges at 500–1500m alt., the plants shrinking and becoming almost subterranean in dry times. Mature plants can be 10–15cm across. When well grown they have plump tubercles and dense clumps of white wool. Showy pink flowers, up to 5cm across, appear in summer.

Ariocarpus retusus Living Rock Cactus

Although the fastest grower in the genus, this species can still take 10 years or more to flower. Occurring in scattered populations in parts of Mexico, this species is quite variable with the plants ranging in colour from grey to bluish or yellowish-green. Its stem, which can reach 25cm tall and 30cm wide, emerges well above ground. White, cream or pale yellow flowers open widely on sunny days. This species will tolerate light frost.

ARROJADOA

An interesting genus consisting of five species of columnar cacti from Brazil. The stems grow in spurts, with apical clusters of wool and bristles crowning the top of each season's growth, among which the colourful flowers emerge. Each stem renews growth after flowering is finished, resulting in segmented areas, each segment defined by a collar of hairs. The brightly coloured tubular flowers attract birds. Easy to grow, these cacti need sun, good drainage, good ventilation and dry winter rest. Frost tolerance is variable. Increase by seed and stem cuttings.

Arrojadoa rhodantha

Growing to about 2m tall, this species has weak stems which can gain support by clambering through nearby shrubs. The prominently segmented stems, covered with yellow to brown spines, have apical tufts (actually cephalia) consisting of a mixture of brown wool and bristles. Black buds open to colourful pink to mauve or purple tubular flowers 3–3.5cm long. This species will tolerate light frost.

ASTROPHYTUM

Although there are only five species in this Mexican genus, three exhibit great variation in growth habit and features such as spination, colour and spotting (tufts of short white hairs, sometimes called flakes). The flowers, mostly yellow, have an attractive satin-like sheen. Many cactus enthusiasts specialise in these plants valuing them for their sculptured symmetrical shapes. Usually they are solitary but sometimes a plant offsets to form a clump. They grow well for many years as a container plant, but large plants are sometimes seen planted as landscape subjects in dry gardens. These cacti need excellent drainage, good air movement and winter rest. Some growers use alkaline potting mix for these plants. Frost tolerance is not high. Increase by seed or careful division.

Astrophytum capricorne Goat's Horn Cactus

This species is mostly globe-like although very old specimens can form a column to about 1m tall. The green stems, 10–20cm across, are ornamented with tufts of short white hairs and long thin flexible spines. Scented yellow flowers 5–6cm across, with a contrasting red throat, are produced at intervals in summer. Young plants sometimes lack spines and the degree of spotting (hair tufts) varies greatly between plants.

Astrophytum myriostigma Bishop's Cap

Prized for its stone-like symmetrical spineless stems which can reach 25×18cm, this species is mostly solitary, but sometimes offsets to form a clump. A wonderful potplant that achieves its best appearance in the bright filtered light of a glasshouse, this species is available in various forms ranging from green (hairless) variants to silver-grey plants covered with numerous flakes. Variation is also exhibited in the number (four to ten) of ribs, their shape and angularity. One special collector's item has twisted ribs. A tall growing variant is also grown. Shiny lemon yellow to bright yellow flowers are produced at intervals in summer.

Astrophytum myriostigma

Arrojadoa rhodantha

Tony Wood

Ariocarpus retusus

Astrophytum ornatum hybrid

Tony Wood

Astrophytum ornatum var. *glabrescens*

Astrophytum capricorne

Carnegiea gigantea

Astrophytum ornatum Monk's Hood Cactus

The stems of this species are dark green, variously dotted with white hair tufts (sometimes the tufts are in bands) and deeply ribbed with short stout spines. Young plants are globe-like but old specimens can form a broad column in excess of 1m tall and 30cm wide. Shiny cream to yellow flowers open widely on warm sunny days. Many variants and hybrids of this species are grown including some with bright green stems totally lacking hair tufts (var. *glabrescens*).

CARNEGIEA

The single species in this genus, which is native to the Sonoran Desert, extending from Arizona through southern California into Mexico, is one of the best known and largest members of the cactus family. Often a prominent feature of cowboy films, it is easily recognised by its broad, spiny, ribbed stems and characteristic upward-curving branches. Large, funnel-shaped, bat-pollinated flowers, which open during the day and night, are followed by tasty red fruit that are prized by local residents. It is the state flower of Arizona.

Carnegiea gigantea Saguaro, Giant Cactus

Rarely grown successfully in Australia, this iconic species is still nevertheless frequently seen as small potted plants in cactus collections. Young seedlings rot easily and even established plants are very slow growing. They are sometimes grafted onto *Trichocereus spachianus* in an attempt to overcome these difficulties. This species needs excellent drainage, warmth and low humidity. Arid inland climates, such as found at Lightning Ridge in northern NSW, have proved to be amenable to this species and here there are several large specimens in the collection at Bevan's Cactus Gardens, Lightning Ridge.

CEPHALOCEREUS

There are five species in this genus of columnar cacti, all native to southern Mexico. The ribbed stems of these large cacti are densely covered with bristle-like or hair-like spines. Tubular or bell-shaped flowers open at night, arising from woolly or hairy areoles. These cacti need excellent drainage, good air movement and dry winter rest. Frost tolerance is not high. Increase by seed or stem cuttings.

Cephalocereus senilis Old Man of Mexico, Bunny Cactus

A popular but slow growing Mexican cactus which is best grown in the ground, but also does well for many years as a potted plant. Old plants can reach in excess of 10m tall with the slender columnar stems (10–12cm across) covered with grey to white soft hairs that conceal sharp spines. Whitish, yellowish or pinkish funnel-shaped flowers about 7cm across are produced nocturnally from among hairy patches (pseudocephalia) near the top of the taller stems in summer. It has been reported that a plant grown at Tennyson in Victoria produced its first flowers after 40 years.

CEREUS

This generic name, one of the earliest used for cacti, has been applied to most of the columnar cacti at some stage. Modern interpretations suggest that the genus contains some 34 species of shrubby or tree-like cacti from eastern parts of South America and the Caribbean region, although there is still confusion as to the correct application of some names. A few species are widely grown for their edible fruit. Many also have excellent sculptural outlines and are useful in larger gardens and as feature plants in the landscape. Their large white or reddish flowers open only at night. Monstrose forms of at least one species are commonly grown as novelties. Frost tolerance is variable but many species are quite frost tolerant. Increase by seed and stem cuttings.

Tony Wood

Cephalocereus senilis

Cephalocereus senilis

Cereus hildmannianus Hedge Cactus, Queen of the Night

Commonly planted for its sculptural qualities, this large, strongly branching cactus forms a dense, hedge-like clump 5–10m tall and several metres across. The thick bluish green to greyish green stems grow in spurts with a constriction between each phase. Large white nocturnal flowers 20–25cm across are followed by plump red fruit 4–5cm long which have a tasty white pulp. Best in full sun, this easily grown species will withstand heavy frost. The typical subspecies (subsp. *hildmannianus* from Brazil, Paraguay, Uruguay and Argentina) is spineless whereas subsp. *uruguayensis* (from Uruguay) has spines along the ribs. Several monstrose forms of this cactus are grown (another photo page 22).

Cereus hildmannianus 'Knobby Monstrose form'

Cereus hildmannianus subsp. *hildmannianus, flower*

Cereus hildmannianus subsp. *hildmannianus*

Cereus hildmannianus subsp. *uruguayensis*

Cereus hildmannianus subsp. *uruguayensis*

Cereus validus

Native to Bolivia and Argentina, this slow-growing species (usually sold as *Cereus forbesii*) forms a clump of sparsely spiny ribbed bluish to greenish stems 1–3m tall. Reddish or white flowers about 10cm across are followed by small red fruit. This species will tolerate light to moderate frost.

CLEISTOCACTUS

There are about 48 species in this widely distributed South American genus, many growing among shrubs and boulders at relatively high altitude. Mostly slender-stemmed (30–45mm across) and covered with thin flexible spines, these cacti branch freely to form clumps. The nectar-rich often zygomorphic flowers, many of which appear like colourful narrow tubes, are produced freely (especially in cold areas) at any time, sometimes in sporadic bursts. Popular in cultivation, these easily grown cacti are excellent for the beginner. They grow best in a sunny position with good air movement. Most will tolerate frost, although the growing tips can be killed by heavy frost. Although very tolerant of dryness, these plants respond well to summer watering. Increase by seed, division and stem cuttings.

Cleistocactus buchtienii

Native to Bolivia, this species grows in open areas of stony ground in the mountains at more than 3000m alt. The stems (to 1.5m long), which can be erect or sprawling, are covered with yellowish brown spines. Bright red to pinkish tubular flowers to 6cm long (which barely open) appear mainly in winter–spring.

Cleistocactus hyalacanthus

A relatively fast-growing species from Bolivia and Argentina that reaches about 1m tall, the thin stems densely covered with fine bristle-like whitish or brownish spines. Bright red tubular flowers (about 4cm long) that barely open appear in winter–spring.

Cereus validus

Cleistocactus buchtienii

Cleistocactus hyalacanthus flowers

Cleistocactus hyalacanthus

Cleistocactus ritteri

Cleistocactus ritteri flowers

Cleistocactus samaipatanus

Cleistocactus sepium

Cleistocactus ritteri

An interesting Bolivian species with slender branching green stems to about 1m tall covered with white to yellowish spines. Greenish yellow to pale yellow or red tubular flowers about 4cm long are produced in groups, mainly during winter and spring.

Cleistocactus samaipatanus

Popular for its colourful floral displays produced at intervals over summer and autumn, this Bolivian species is also easy to grow. The red flowers, tubular at the base, have numerous narrow petals that spread widely or even recurve. They are carried on upright or decumbent stems to 1.5m tall covered with yellow to brown spines. A crested form is available. Mature plants will tolerate frost, but small plants need protection.

Cleistocactus sepium

Growing to about 1.5m tall, this Ecuadorian species is valued for its spring and summer displays of bright red flowers, each flower up to 8cm long and of a similar width. The stems, which are often dark green, have wavy ribs and prominent pale spines. Globular fruit are pale green to yellowish when ripe.

Cleistocactus strausii Silver Torch Cactus, Snow Pole

A very distinctive clumping species from Bolivia that has thick stems (to 2.5m tall) densely covered with silvery-white spines. Dark red tubular flowers 8–9cm long, that barely expand at the tip, are produced at intervals from autumn to spring. Mostly cold-hardy, once established (seedlings can be damaged by frost), it provides an excellent focal point in a cactus garden. The tall stems are easily broken by strong wind. This popular cactus is usually available from specialist growers. A crested form is sometimes grown.

Cleistocactus strausii

Cleistocactus tupizensis

Cleistocactus winteri flowers

Cleistocactus winteri

Tony Wood

Copiapoa bridgesii

Cleistocactus tupizensis

Growing about 1m tall, this Bolivian species has stems about 6cm thick covered with whitish to pale brown spines. Curved red tubular flowers (6–8cm long) produce an interesting display in winter-spring.

Cleistocactus winteri

Best displayed in a hanging basket, this freely branching Bolivian cactus, has slender sprawling to pendulous stems to 1m long covered with short golden spines. The stems (about 2.5cm across) grow to 1m long. Colourful flowers (pink to orange-red), each about 4cm across, are produced in flushes during spring and summer. Each flower lasts a few days. Cold hardy and easily grown, this species can also be effectively planted among large rocks and used as a groundcover. Plants in very dry areas may need extra water in winter to prevent stem dieback. An attractive crested form is also available.

COPIAPOA

A genus of 26 species of relatively easily grown decorative cacti, all from Chile, mostly from desert regions in the north where they receive all or most of their water from fogs. They range from solitary plants to clumpers, with some species forming extensive spreading clumps in the wild. Most species have strongly ribbed globose stems with woolly tips, but some become cylindrical with age. Yellow (sometimes tinged with pink or red) funnel-shaped flowers open during the day in the warmer months, particularly spring and late summer-autumn. Of variable growth rate and often displaying great variation within a species, these ornamental cacti need excellent drainage and good air movement. Allow the soil mix to dry out between waterings. Some species will tolerate winter watering. Frost tolerance is not high. Increase by seed or careful division.

Copiapoa bridgesii

This solitary or clumping species has bright green cylindrical stems 20–30cm or more tall, with a white-woolly apex. Generally well armed with long spines, this cactus often holds the apical spines erect. Pale yellow to bright yellow flowers add to the decorative appeal. Clumping specimens can be distinctive, often developing the outer stems in an appealing upwards curve.

Copiapoa calderana

A variable species that occurs naturally among rocks in gravelly soil in rocky coastal sites. The plants, which have a long tuberous root, are globose when young, becoming cylindrical with age. Mostly slow growing, the plants of this species range in colour from bright green to bluish grey. Partial shade rather than full sun may be best for this species.

Copiapoa cinerea

A slow-growing solitary or clumping species (to 1m tall) that has round to cylindrical, deeply ribbed stems that are usually chalky-white to ash-grey, although green-stemmed plants are known. This colouration is from a waxy secretion that develops best in sunlight (cherished plants have a strong waxy covering). The stems carry blackish spines, although spineless forms are known. Exposure to sunlight is generally necessary to promote flowering. Protect from frost.

Tony Wood

Copiapoa calderana

Tony Wood

Copiapoa calderana flower

Tony Wood

Copiapoa cinerea

Tony Wood

Copiapoa coquimbana

Copiapoa coquimbana

Plants of this species in nature are often seen in large clumps, but cultivated plants are generally quite slow growing. The stems, which range from globose to cylindrical and from green to glaucous, are covered with pale to blackish spines. Yellow or reddish bell-shaped flowers are produced from the woolly area at the top of each stem. Protect from frost.

Copiapoa krainziana

A slow-growing decorative species that eventually forms a compact clump, the individual stems mostly hidden by long white flexible spines. Each stem has a woolly crown from which the yellow flowers emerge. Grafting can be used to improve growth rate. Partial shade rather than full sun may be best for this species.

Copiapoa malletiana

A variable species with green to grey cylindrical stems and black needle-like spines. It branches freely and although slow growing can eventually form mound-like patches to about 1m tall and 2m or more wide. Protect from frost.

Copiapoa marginata

Some forms of this variable species are strongly armed with nearly overlapping groups of spreading grey spines, others are much less spiny. A short woody taproot supports the cylindrical stems that widen upwards. Yellow or red-stained yellow flowers open during spring and summer.

Copiapoa mollicula

A clumping but slow-growing species that develops a thick woody taproot and produces offsets from the base and along the stems. Some variants have low stems barely exceeding ground level, others develop shortly erect cylindrical stems. Grafting can be used to improve growth rate. Protect from frost.

Copiapoa taltalensis

A free-flowering species that forms clumps to 50cm tall, each supported by fleshy tuberous roots. Easily grown, this species can flower when quite young, the pale yellow, slightly fragrant flowers often produced at intervals over summer. It is sometimes used as a grafting stock for slow-growing *Copiapoa* species.

Copiapoa coquimbana

Tony Wood

Copiapoa krainziana

Tony Wood

Copiapoa malletiana

Tony Wood

Copiapoa marginata

Tony Wood

Copiapoa taltalensis

Copiapoa mollicula
photo Tony Wood

CORRYOCACTUS

This is a genus of about 12 species of shrubby cacti from South America that branch freely from the base to form erect or sprawling clumps. The plants have slender spiny stems and produce showy bright-coloured flowers in shades of yellow, orange, red or purple during summer. The flowers, which open during the day, have a short tubular base covered with scales. Globose spiny fruit are juicy and tasty to eat. These cacti are best grown in a large container or in the ground. They need excellent drainage, bright light, good air movement and dry winter rest. Most will tolerate cold and light frost. Increase by seed or stem cuttings.

Corryocactus melanotrichus

Corryocactus melanotrichus

Native to the Bolivian Andes (2500–3000m alt.), this species forms erect clumps of slender spiny stems 2–4m tall, the plants sometimes scrambling through adjacent shrubs. The pale spines (1–2cm long) contrast with the bright green stems. Bright red to purplish-red widely-opening flowers 5–6cm across in summer are followed by round spiny fruit. This species will tolerate light frost.

CORYPHANTHA

This popular genus (USA and Mexico) consists of about 43 species of small solitary and clumping cacti with a neat growth habit and attractive large flowers. Some species flower in late summer when few other cacti are out. Globe-like to elongate cylindrical stems are covered with small grooved nipple-like structures (called tubercles) carrying apical spines. Wool develops in the grooves and some species also have nectar-secreting glands located on the tubercles. The flowers arise between the young tubercles at the stem apex. Many species are easily grown and are excellent for the beginner. Best grown in a relatively deep container, these cacti, some of which are fast growers, need excellent drainage, bright light (some in full sun), good air movement and dry winter rest. Repot every two to three years. Some will tolerate cold, even frost; others need warmth. Increase by seed or careful division.

Coryphantha calipensis Snow Cap Cactus

The stem apex of this Mexican species is often covered with a tuft of white woolly hairs giving rise to the common name. Clumping with dark olive-green stems to 9cm long and wide, it has prominent conical tubercles tipped with needle-like spines. The plants produce dark-centred cream to yellow flowers in spring and summer. This species needs protection from frost.

Coryphantha cornifera Rhinoceros Cactus

Usually solitary, this Mexican species has an ovoid stem 10–12cm tall and up to 15cm across, prominent grey-white spines (often without any central spines) and cream to yellow flowers (sometimes red) 5–7cm across. Ovoid fleshy green fruit often develop after flowering. Best in full sun or bright light, this species is tolerant of light frosts but can be prone to root rot if the drainage is at all suspect.

Tony Wood

Coryphantha calipensis

Tony Wood

Coryphantha cornifera

Coryphantha echinoidea

A small solitary species from Mexico that has a bright green globe-like to cylindrical stem 5–6cm tall bearing groups of stiff spreading radial spines, the central spines often only developing near the top of the plant. Lovely cream to yellow flowers open widely on warm spring days. Although easily grown, sooty mould developing on the nectar, which exudes from its tubercle glands can mar its appearance.

Coryphantha elephantidens

Solitary or more usually forming a large clump, this Mexican species has dark green shiny globose stems with the spines confined to the tips of the large tubercles. Tufts of snowy white hairs can be prominent on the stem tips. Decorative flowers, 8–10cm across, in a range of colours including pink or purple and white or yellow with reddish markings in the throat, are produced in spring.

Coryphantha radians Sea Urchin Cactus

Usually solitary, but occasionally forming offsets, this Mexican species has small green stems that are covered with groups of closely appressed spines (usually no central spines occur). Large yellow funnel-shaped flowers (7–10cm across), sometimes with a red base, appear in spring and at intervals over summer.

Coryphantha ramillosa Big Bend Cory Cactus

Occurring on limestone formations, this rare and threatened species, from Texas and Mexico, is usually solitary, but can also produce offsets. Grey-green stems (to 9cm tall and 10cm wide), which are often widest toward the top, are covered with pale radial spines and curved or twisted central spines. Lovely bright pink to purple flowers 3–5cm across are produced in late spring and summer.

DENMOZA

The single species in this genus grows naturally in the foothills of the Andes in Argentina. It is a slow-growing solitary cactus with unusual tubular flowers that open during the day. It needs excellent drainage, full sun, good air movement and dry winter rest. Increase by seed.

Tony Wood

Coryphantha echinoidea

Paul Forster

Coryphantha elephantidens

Tony Wood

Coryphantha radians

Tony Wood

Coryphantha ramillosa

Tony Wood

Denmoza rhodacantha

Paul Forster

Echinocactus grusonii, white spined variant

Echinocactus grusonii. multiheaded plant

Echinocactus grusonii, flowers

Denmoza rhodacantha

This cactus changes with age, being globe-like for many years before developing into a barrel shape. Old plants can reach 1.5m tall and 30cm across. Young plants are covered with attractive red spines, becoming grey in older plants. Curved red flowers 5–7cm long appear near the stem apex of older plants. This species will tolerate light frost.

ECHINOCACTUS

Although more than 1000 botanical names have been applied to this genus, modern studies show that it consists of only six species. Distributed from southern USA to Mexico, these solitary or clumping cacti have ribbed globe-like to cylindrical stems with stout spines and woolly tops. Smallish bell-shaped flowers nestle among the apical wool of mature plants (photo page 14). These cacti need excellent drainage, partial sun to full sun, good air movement and dry winter rest. Some will tolerate cold, even frost, others need warmth. Increase by seed or careful division.

Echinocactus grusonii Golden Barrel Cactus

Young plants of this popular cactus have long golden yellow spines, whereas mature plants have shorter darker spines. Although critically endangered in the wild, this cactus is widely grown in many countries where it is commonly seen in cactus collections and planted in groups as a landscape subject. Growing to more than 1m tall and 80cm wide, the mature plants form a large, ribbed, globe-like stem. Yellow flowers, which are produced only on the larger plants, develop in rows around the woolly crown. Easily grown this species will tolerate full sun and moderate frost. In winter, growers in cold climates cover the growing point with plastic or bubble wrap to keep moisture out and prevent freezing in frosty weather. A distinctive form with white spines is available.

Echinocactus grusonii

Echinocactus platyacanthus Giant Barrel Cactus

A massive cactus with a barrel-like stem that can grow up to 2.5m tall and more than 1m wide. The stem of a mature plant, which ranges from yellowish-green to bluish-grey, has a flattish or saddle-like top and numerous deep ribs that carry groups of sturdy, flattish, strongly banded spines. By contrast seedlings look very different as they have very few ribs and prominent tubercles. Groups of bright yellow flowers, each flower about 7cm wide, emerge from the woolly apex of mature plants in late spring and over summer. Although easy, this cactus is a very slow grower. Frost is best avoided and it must be kept dry over winter.

ECHINOCEREUS

Recognised by its large colourful flowers with green stigma lobes (sometimes white), this popular genus consists of about 60 species distributed in western parts of the USA and Mexico. They are mostly clumping, with globe-like to cylindrical ribbed stems, sometimes armed with long spines (in some species the spines change colour with the season). The stems of some species clamber through surrounding shrubs. The flowers open widely during the day, sometimes producing a spectacular display. Generally easy to grow and relatively fast, these can be grown in a container or dry garden. They need bright light (some tolerate full sun), good air movement and dry, cool winter rest. Some of these cacti will only flower after they have been through a cold frosty winter. Species with pectinate spines (such as *E. pectinatus*) can be prone to attack by spider mites). Increase by seed, careful division or stem cuttings.

Echinocereus adustus

Native to rocky slopes and high alt. deserts in Mexico above 1800m alt., this species usually develops a solitary cylindrical stem 10–20cm tall adorned with rows of pectinate spines (which show considerable variation in number and form). Lovely magenta to purplish pink funnel-shaped flowers 5–6cm across open widely on warm days in late spring and summer. Easy to grow and an ideal cactus for the beginner, this species will tolerate moderately heavy frost.

Echinocereus cinerascens

A Mexican species with sprawling to decumbent stems that branch freely, eventually forming a mound of crowded growths. The stems, bright green, cylindrical and with prominent tubercles, have sharp thin spines often in the form of a cross.

Paul Forster

Echinocactus platyacanthus seedling

Paul Forster

Echinocactus platyacanthus

Echinocereus adustus

Echinocereus cinerascens

Paul Forster

Echinocereus engelmannii Sonoran Desert

Echinocereus engelmannii

Michael Mathieson

Echinocereus knippelianus

Lovely magenta-pink flowers 10–12cm across with a pale throat open widely on spring days, each flower arising towards the base of a growth. This species will tolerate light frost.

Echinocereus engelmannii Strawberry Hedgehog Cactus

A well-armed cactus that originates from south-western USA and adjacent parts of Mexico. The plants form crowded clumps of cylindrical stems to 50cm tall covered with overlapping spines to 2cm long. Bright pink to magenta or purplish red flowers 6–7cm across open in spring and early summer towards the top of the stems. This species will tolerate light frost.

Echinocereus enneacanthus Banana Cactus

Excellent for a dry sunny position, this cactus, which is from Texas and Mexico, develops into a clump of sprawling to upright pale green stems to 1m tall, each stem (often wrinkly) to about 10cm thick. Shiny flowers of a brilliant magenta-pink colouration (sometimes reddish) open widely on sunny days in spring and early summer. This species will tolerate light to moderate frost.

Echinocereus enneacanthus

Echinocereus knippelianus

A slow-growing species that offsets and eventually forms a large clump. Individual stems, globose and dark green, have five to seven broad ribs and sparse spines. Funnel-shaped white to pale pink or purplish flowers, up to 6cm diameter, open in spring. Native to Mexico, it grows in mountainous regions above 2000m alt. This easily grown species tolerates light to moderate frost.

Echinocereus longisetus

A robust species that branches freely to form a spreading clump. Large, old plants can be up to 1m across with slender erect to sprawling stems covered with spines and long white bristly hairs. Spring and summer displays of purple flowers, each flower 6–7cm across, are produced from the basal parts of each stem. This Mexican species, which occurs naturally from about 800m to more than 1800m alt., should be grown in full sun and will tolerate quite heavy frost. The subsp. *delaetii* has curly, hair-like bristles. Requires cold frosty winters to flower.

Echinocereus nivosus

Although restricted naturally to steep rocky slopes at about 2000m alt. in Mexico, this species adapts well to cultivation and will tolerate light to moderate frost. It is best in full sun in an airy location. A mounding cactus, its stems are covered with needle-like white spines. Colourful displays of pink to mauve or magenta flowers in spring and summer make this cactus highly sought after by collectors.

Echinocereus papillosus Yellow Alicoche

Growing to about 1m tall and with individual stems erect to sprawling and 3–5cm thick, this cactus forms a crowded clump. Cream to yellow flowers 8–10cm across with an orange to red throat open on sunny days in spring. This species will tolerate light to moderate frost.

Echinocereus pectinatus Lace Cactus

A distinctive cactus with its cylindrical stems, to 20 × 5cm, covered with rows of whitish interlaced comb-like spines. Mostly solitary, this popular species, native to southern Texas and Mexico, produces funnel-shaped pink flowers (with a white throat) 10–15cm across at intervals in spring and summer. This species tolerates light frost.

Echinocereus longisetus subsp. *delaetii*

Echinocereus nivosus

Echinocereus papillosus

Echinocereus pectinatus

Echinocereus polyacanthus

Echinocereus pentalophus subsp. *procumbens*

Echinocereus pentalophus Lady Finger Cactus

This cactus, widely distributed in southern Texas and Mexico, has slender, erect to sprawling cylindrical stems and showy purplish-pink flowers (10–12cm across) with a white or yellow throat. Best in sun, it will tolerate light frost. The subsp. *procumbens* is ideal for a hanging basket where the creeping stems and colourful flowers can be shown to advantage. Tolerates light frost.

Echinocereus polyacanthus Claret-cup Cactus

Occurring in Mexico, New Mexico and Arizona, this cactus forms large spreading clumps with bright green to pale green, spiny cylindrical stems (15–30cm long) that taper to the apex. Displays of colourful orange to red flowers are produced at the stem tips during spring and early summer. This species tolerates light frost.

Echinocereus poselgeri

Native to Mexico and Texas, this unusual cactus has a sprawling or climbing habit, the thin stems threading through adjacent shrubs. The sparsely branched stems, which arise from a tuberous rootstock, can grow to more than 1m tall. Cream to bright pink widely opening flowers appear at or near the stem tips in spring, each flower lasting a few days, and closing each night.

Echinocereus rigidissimus Arizona Rainbow Cactus

Grown as much for its attractive spines as well as its large colourful flowers, this species is native to south-western parts of the USA and adjacent areas of Mexico. Mostly solitary, it forms a cylindrical stem to 30 × 10cm that is covered with closely appressed interlaced spines. Spine colour ranges from yellow to red and brown, with seasonal changes adding to the appeal. Brilliant purple flowers with white throats open in spring. This species, which can be difficult to grow, will tolerate light to moderate frost.

Echinocereus poselgeri

Echinocereus scheerii

The stems of this clumping species, which is from north-western Mexico, can spread with a sprawling habit or be upright. Reaching up to 70cm long, the stems have prominent blunt ribs and pale spines. Large colourful flowers (orange, red, scarlet or pink) arise from the sides of the stems in spring and summer. This attractive species should be grown in full sun and will tolerate quite heavy frost if dry. The subsp. *gentryi* has pink flowers with a paler throat.

Echinocereus subinermis

Distinctive for the strongly ribbed bluish green globose stems and prized for its displays of large (10–12cm across) yellow flowers, this Mexican cactus also has the virtue of being easy to grow and nearly spineless. It is best grown in a pot where it is sheltered from excessive hot sun and severe frost.

Echinocereus triglochidiatus Claret-cup Cactus

A variable species that forms crowded mounds of prickly bluish green stems to 1m wide and 40cm high. Displays of cup-shaped orange to scarlet flowers, each 5–7cm across, transform the clumps at intervals in spring and summer. Excellent for a dry garden, this species will tolerate light frosts.

Echinocereus subinermis

Echinocereus viridiflorus Green Hedgehog Cactus

Widely distributed in desert regions of the southern states of the USA and northern Mexico, this cold-hardy cactus is easily grown in a pot or dry garden. Ranging from small globe-like stems to short cylinders (to 10cm tall) with colourful spines, this solitary species produces its lemon-scented green flowers during late spring and summer. The subsp. *chloranthus*, which has a cylindrical stem, is very free flowering, producing attractive floral displays.

Paul Forster

Echinocereus scheerii subsp. *gentryi*

Michael Mathieson

Echinocereus rigidissimus

Echinocereus triglochidiatus

Echinocereus viridiflorus subsp. *viridiflorus*

Echinocereus websterianus

The cylindrical to column-like stems of this prized cactus (to 50cm tall) are usually covered with golden spines, but these are occasionally white. Clumping in habit and generally slow growing, it offsets freely, the stems mostly erect but sometimes sprawling. Pink funnel-shaped flowers 3–4cm across open in spring.

Echinocereus viridiflorus subsp. *chloranthus*

Echinocereus websterianus

ECHINOPSIS

Echinopsis ancistrophora subsp. *arachnacantha*

Named for their dense covering of spines (likened to a sea urchin or hedgehog), this confusing genus includes about 85 species of cacti from South America. Members of this genus can be difficult to recognise because of the wide range of characters encompassed within the group. Until recently the widely grown genus *Trichocereus* was included here, along with *Helianthocereus, Soehrensia*, *Lobivia* and some others. A recent detailed study, however, has again segregated *Trichocereus* as distinct, with *Helianthocereus* a synonym. Most of the revised *Echinopsis* group are globe-like, with spiny ribs prized for their large, showy, colourful, but often short-lived diurnal flowers (most last one day). Some are solitary, others form clumps. Provide excellent drainage, good air movement and dry winter rest. Some will tolerate full sun but most (especially the small growers) respond to shade during the hottest part of summer days. Several species will tolerate cold, even frost, others need warmth. Increase by seed or careful division. This genus is enhanced by a range of easily grown hybrids that produce large colourful flowers (see last entry).

Echinopsis ancistrophora

An easily grown species that is ideal for the beginner. Under good conditions it is quite fast growing, freely clumping and quickly filling a pot with shiny, dark green globose stems. Showy flowers with a long basal tube produce colourful displays during spring and summer. Opening to about 5cm across, the flowers can be in a range of colours including white, yellow, orange, pink and red. Protect the plants from excessively hot sun. Will tolerate light to moderate frost. The subsp. *arachnacantha* is smaller growing with yellow flowers; subsp. *cardenasiana* has violet-pink to red flowers.

Echinopsis ancistrophora subsp. *ancistrophora*

Echinopsis ancistrophora subsp. *cardenasiana*

Echinopsis aurea

Echinopsis aurea

This Argentinian cactus, solitary or clumping, has deeply ribbed globe-like or short column-like stems 4–6cm across and up to 10cm tall, covered with brown spines. Shiny cream to yellow flowers (sometimes pink to purple), each 6–8cm across, are produced freely at intervals in spring.

Echinopsis backebergii

A variable species that is native to Bolivia and Peru. Solitary or clumping, it has globose to shortly cylindrical bright green stems to 8cm tall that are deeply ribbed and ornamented with short to long (5cm) spines. Funnel-shaped flowers 5–9cm across produce attractive displays at intervals in spring and summer. Floral colours include pink, red and purple, often with a paler central area. This species will tolerate light frost.

Echinopsis bruchii

A commonly grown cactus that can be successful in a dry garden or pot. The plants, which are usually solitary, are heavily ribbed and covered with brownish spines. They can reach up to 50cm across and will tolerate light frost. Bright red flowers 4–5cm across open during the day in spring and summer.

Tony Wood

Echinopsis backebergii

Echinopsis bruchii

Echinopsis chamaecereus

Echinopsis chamaecereus in basket

Echinopsis chamaecereus Peanut Cactus

Ideal for the novice grower, this rewarding little Argentinian cactus reproduces freely to form expanding clumps. The stems, which are not very prickly, can be easily separated to begin a new plant. Attractive orange-red flowers, large for the size of the plant, open widely in spring and summer to produce an arresting display. 'Aureus', is a yellow-stemmed cultivar lacking chlorophyll and propagated by grafting (photo page 22).

Echinopsis cinnabarina

This cold, hardy cactus is found naturally at 2000–4000m alt. in the Andes mountains of Bolivia. Solitary or clumping, it forms dark green stems to 15cm across. Dark red to scarlet flowers, each about 4cm across, arise near the stem apex during late spring and summer. Can burn in hot summer sun. Suitable for a pot or garden.

Echinopsis famatimensis Orange Cob Cactus

The short cylindrical stems of this cactus, which is from above 2500m alt. in the mountains of Argentina, are covered with a network of closely embracing comb-like whitish spines. Mainly solitary, this slow-growing species, which is susceptible to root rot, is well known for its brilliant displays of yellow to orange or purple flowers that expand from woolly buds in summer–autumn. Tolerates light frost.

Echinopsis oxygona Easter Lily Cactus

Extremely tolerant of neglect, this free-flowering cactus, which occurs naturally in several South American countries, is one of the best for the novice grower. A fast-grower that will soon fill a pot, this species probably does best in a well-drained garden. It looks appealing among rocks and tolerates full summer sunshine and winter frost. The lovely pink or white flowers, 16–20cm long, last about 24 hours after opening in an evening. An adaptable crested form is also grown. This crest, which can be grown successfully on its own roots, also produces flowers.

Echinopsis saltensis

This species, which is from northern Argentina, is valued for its neat growth habit and displays of blood red flowers. Usually solitary, this species has a taproot and globose stems about 10cm across. The flowers, which arise low down on the sides of a stem in spring, are 4–5cm across. This species will tolerate light frost.

Echinopsis cinnabarina

Echinopsis famatimensis

Echinopsis subdenudata, clump

Echinopsis subdenudata Bald Hedgehog Cactus

This relatively small cactus always demands attention at flowering time because of the disproportionately large flowers (about 20cm long) that arise from the nearly spineless stems. Unfortunately the snowy white flowers (sometimes pink) last only about one day after opening in the late afternoon. Native to Bolivia and Paraguay this easily grown species will tolerate light frost.

Echinopsis subdenudata

Echinopsis saltensis

Echinopsis subdenudata pink form

Echinopsis oxygona

ECHINOPSIS HYBRIDS

American hybridists have been breeding *Echinopsis* (including *Lobivia* and other relatives) since the 1930s, with some startling results. The first to be produced were a series of Paramount hybrids bred in California in the 1930–40s by Harry Johnson. These were followed by a further range of hybrids produced by Bob Schick (appropriately named the Schick hybrids). About 35 Paramount hybrids were named and more than 200 Schick cultivars are known. A group of hybrids, known as the Sussex Hybrids have also been produced in England. Nowadays more than 800 hybrids have been registered. A few Paramount hybrids are available in Australia, but cultivars from the other breeding programs appear to be lacking. These hybrids are valued for their ease of culture and the ability to produce several floral displays each season. Although only lasting about 24 hours, the large and often brilliantly coloured flowers are very showy. Mostly these plants will tolerate frost and sun, but some need protection from the heat of summer days. They are good garden plants in drier areas, but in wetter climates the plants may split badly after taking up too much water.

Echinopsis hybrid 'Peach Monarch'

Echinopsis hybrid 'Salmon Queen'

Echinopsis hybrid 'Stars & Stripes'

Echinopsis hybrid 'White Knight'

Echinopsis hybrid 'Golden Glory'

EPITHELANTHA

A recent revision shows there are six species in this genus of variable miniature cacti. Native to south-western USA and adjacent parts of Mexico, they grow in rocky areas between 600 and 2300m alt. They are solitary or clumping cacti with very small globose growths covered neatly with closely appressed spines. The small flowers, which arise from the tips of the areoles, are followed by thin red fruit. These cacti are relatively easy to grow but can be prone to rotting and need excellent drainage in an open airy position. They tolerate sun and light to moderate frost. Increase by seed.

Epithelantha unguispina Button Cactus, Ping Pong Ball Cactus

This species, previously treated as a subspecies of *E. micromeris*, grows among limestone rocks. It is restricted to a small area in Mexico. Usually clumping, the compact ping pong ball–like growths are only 2–6cm across. They are covered with ashy white spines and in late winter-spring carry inconspicuous pale pink flowers near the centre of the growth. Cylindrical bright pink to red fruit 1–2cm long form a conspicuous display after the flowers.

ERIOSYCE

A genus of 35 species of small cacti from arid desert regions of South America, often at high alt. A number of these cacti are true dwarfs and many have a swollen tap root. They have ribbed stems and spines carried on the tips of tubercles. The attractive flowers open during the day. Unusually the fruit are hollow with loose seeds, opening near the base when ripe.

Generally easy to grow but prone to rotting, these cacti are best grown in a pot with an open, freely draining mix. They also need sun or bright light, good ventilation and winter dormancy. Many will tolerate frost for short periods. Increase by seed or stem cuttings.

Eriosyce chilensis

Solitary or clumping, this Chilean species is popular for its attractive pink to red flowers held upright from the stem tips in spring and summer. Growing to about 1m tall, the stems have numerous notched ribs and stiff yellowish to brownish spines. The var. *albidiflora* has yellow flowers marked with red. Tolerates light to moderate frost.

Epithelantha unguispina

Eriosyce chilensis var. *albidiflora*

Eriosyce kunzei

A commonly grown, but variable cactus from low alt. in the mountains of Chile. Usually solitary, it has a globe-like or domed growth covered with thin to stout spines. Attractive funnel-shaped pink to brownish flowers (often with darker central bands) 3–3.5cm across are produced among the upper spines in spring and summer. Tolerates light frost.

Tony Wood

Eriosyce kunzei

Michael Mathieson

Eriosyce senilis

Eriosyce subgibbosa

Tony Wood

Escobaria albicolumnaria

Michael Mathieson

Eriosyce subgibbosa

Eriosyce senilis

A solitary species from near-coastal valleys in Chile. It has a large taproot and globose to cylindrical stems densely covered with needle-like spines. Groups of colourful funnel-shaped flowers are produced at the top of the growth in spring. Flower colour ranges from pink to carmine but some variants have paler central tones giving a multicoloured effect. Protect from frost.

Eriosyce subgibbosa

A solitary or sparsely offsetting species from coastal habitats in Chile. Young stems are round but elongate and become cylindrical with age, often leaning or growing along the ground in old plants. The stems have well-developed tubercles and pale stiff needle-like spines. Pink to red flowers are followed by sausage-shaped red fruit. Tolerates light frost only.

ESCOBARIA

There are 23 species of small cacti in this genus that is distributed from southern Canada to northern Mexico, with a single species in Cuba. Solitary or clumping, they have densely spiny smooth ribless stems and tubercles which can become corky with age and may be shed from older parts of the stems. Small diurnal flowers with fringed petals are produced from the top of the stems in spring. Several species are popular with hobbyists. They can be grown in a pot of well-drained mix in bright light or sun. A couple of cold-hardy species (*C. missouriensis* and *C. vivipara*) will tolerate heavy frost and can be planted out in temperate gardens. Increase by seed or stem cuttings.

Escobaria albicolumnaria Silver-lace Cob Cactus

Usually solitary, this cactus, native to Texas in the USA, has a shortly cylindrical stem (covered with whitish spines) to 20cm tall and about 6cm across. Small pink funnel-shaped flowers open widely on warm spring days. This species will tolerate light to moderate frost.

Escobaria laredoi

A clumping species from Mexico that forms a crowded cluster of shortly cylindrical slender stems, each densely armed with bristly, stiff, straight or curved, white spines. Purplish, reddish or bright pink flowers about 1cm across appear in spring. Protect from frost.

Escobaria sneedii

A densely clustering cactus from USA (Texas, Florida and New Mexico) where it grows on limestone ridges above 1400m alt. Popular with hobbyists, it can be grown in a pot or planted out in the garden. Some plants consist of a single cylindrical growth with numerous smaller basal offsets, others are just a mass of smallish mostly globular stems (hundreds of stems in old plants). The spines are snowy white and the flowers white to pale pink, sometimes with darker midveins. This species tolerates light to moderate frost.

ESPOSTOA

There are 12 species in this genus of shrubby or tree-like columnar cacti from above 800m alt. in the mountains of Ecuador, Peru and Bolivia. Tall column-like strongly ribbed stems are covered with soft white woolly hairs and short to long spines that emerge through the wool. Densely hairy fertile zones (termed cephalia), that carry the flowers and fruit, develop on the sides of the larger columns. The reddish to white flowers, mostly nocturnal in summer, are followed by juicy green to red fruit. These cacti can be grown in a pot when small but must be repotted frequently and eventually planted out to achieve maturity. Fast growing, they need sun or bright light, good drainage, free ventilation and winter dryness. Many will tolerate frost. Increase by seed or stem cuttings.

Espostoa blossfeldiorum

This cactus often grows as a single stem but sometimes specimens with numerous basal branches are encountered in cultivation. Originating in northern Peru, its slender green stems, which grow 2–4m tall, have glassy needle-like spines and long cephalia comprised of dense patches of glistening grey to yellowish wool. Foul-smelling creamy yellow flowers about 5cm across open at night (closing early next morning), followed by dark green fruit. This species will tolerate light frost only.

Tony Wood

Escobaria laredoi

Tony Wood

Escobaria sneedii

Espostoa blossfeldiorum

Espostoa lanata Peruvian Old Man Cactus, Snowball Cactus

Widely distributed in the Andes of northern Peru and southern Ecuador, this handsome, but slow-growing and variable tree-like cactus, is valued for its woolly covering of white hairs (but with sharp emergent spines). Easily grown, this tall species (2–4m), which gains its best appearance growing in full sun in drier inland areas, will tolerate moderate to heavy frost. Nocturnal white to purple flowers emerge from the thick woolly white to grey cephalia in spring and summer, followed by pink to red fruit. Three subspecies are also cultivated: subsp. *huanucoensis* has yellowish brown felted hairs on the areoles and long white cephalium hairs; subsp. *lanianuligera* has densely packed reddish brown to orange cephalium hairs; subsp. *ruficeps* has dense tufts of rusty brown cephalium wool providing a startling contrast to the rest of the stem.

Espostoa lanata subsp. *lanata* (RHS) subsp. *ruficeps* (LHS)

Espostoa lanata subsp. *lanata* fruit

Espostoa lanata subsp. *lanata*, buds and flower

Espostoa lanata subsp. *lanianuligera*

Espostoopsis dybowskyii

Eulychnia breviflora

ESPOSTOOPSIS

The single species in this genus is an endangered cactus from Brazil. It is grown mainly by hobbyists as a potted plant, but needs to be planted out to achieve maturity. It needs sun or bright light, good drainage, free ventilation and winter dryness. Increase by seed or stem cuttings.

***Espostoopsis dybowskii* Cabega**

Growing 2–4m tall, this shrubby species branches from the base to produce erect columnar stems that are covered with white or silvery wool. The stems appear to grow in spurts and often rings of wool are missing as if brushed off. Yellowish needle-like spines protrude from within the woolly hairs and nocturnal bell-shaped white flowers about 4cm long arise from dense cephalia that resemble tufts of cotton wool. Protect from frost.

EULYCHNIA

This genus consists of five species of tree-like cacti from arid coastal areas of Chile and Peru where extensive coastal fogs provide sufficient moisture for their growth. They are demanding in their requirements of sun, heat, excellent drainage and good ventilation. Allow plants to dry between watering. Frost tolerance is variable. Increase by seed or stem cuttings.

***Eulychnia breviflora* Copao**

The tall stems (2–3m or more) of this handsome cactus are decorated with tufts of pale wool that arise from each areole. They also carry stout spines to 20cm long. Unusual buds densely covered with brown to white wool open to white or pink flowers about 3cm across. This slow-growing cactus adapts well to cultivation given suitable conditions. Best in an open position in full sun. Tolerates light frost.

FACHEIROA

A genus of three species of large, tree-like Brazilian cacti that have spiny columnar stems. Two species develop woolly cephalia near the apex of mature stems. The short-petalled flowers, which open at night, have a basal tube covered with overlapping scales. These cacti can be grown in a pot when small but must be repotted frequently and eventually planted out to achieve maturity. They need sun or bright light, good drainage, winter dryness but will not tolerate frost. Increase by seed or stem cuttings.

Facheiroa cephaliomelana

A large cactus that needs plenty of room to develop fully. Dark green to grey-green strongly ribbed stems, which can grow 2–3.5m tall, are covered with needle-like yellowish spines. Long cephalia bearing yellowish brown hairs develop on one side of the mature stems. Smallish pink flowers develop from the upper part of these hairy patches, opening on summer nights. The flowers are followed by juicy red to purple hairy fruit.

FEROCACTUS

Commonly known as Barrel Cacti from the distinctive shape of their stems, about 30 species of these plants are distributed in the drier regions of south-western USA and Mexico (some on limestone hills). Solitary or clumping and often ferociously armed (many have hooked spines), these cacti range from large globe-like stems to broad cylinders or barrels. The large and often prominent areoles have glands which secrete nectar. Squat flowers are carried near the top of a growth, often in rings, but only on large plants and often only after planting out. Although slow growing, the genus is popular with enthusiasts because of their colourful spines. Many species are easy to grow. They need good drainage, full sun, free air movement and dry winter rest. These cacti need very little water at any time, and it is advisable to avoid watering the stems on hot sunny days as this can lead to sunburn and scarring. Many species will tolerate light frost. Sugary exudates from the areolar nectaries can lead to the development of sooty mould. Some species set masses of fruit which, if they rot, can lead to stem rot or crown rot. Increase is mainly by seed.

Facheiroa cephaliomelana

Paul Forster

Ferocactus echidne

Paul Forster

Ferocactus cylindraceus

Ferocactus cylindraceus California Barrel Cactus

Distributed from southern California and Arizona to Mexico, this massive cactus, which usually consists of a single stem, can reach 3m high and 50cm or more across. Prominent ribs, often with transverse folds, carry straight and hooked spines. Young spines are often red, fading with age. Funnel-shaped yellow flowers are produced on the top of the plant, usually on the side facing the sun. This slow-growing species tolerates light to moderate frost.

Ferocactus echidne Sonoran Barrel Cactus

Native to central Mexico, this handsome species can grow as a solitary stem or develop basal offsets to form a clump. Its deeply ribbed blue-green to grey-green stems, to 40cm × 25cm, have pale spines and terminal clusters of yellow funnel-shaped flowers in spring and summer. It can be grown in a large pot or planted out in the ground. This species will tolerate light frost.

Ferocactus glaucescens

Ferocactus hamatacanthus

Ferocactus herrerae in fruit

Paul Forster

Ferocactus latispinus

Ferocactus glaucescens Blue Barrel Cactus

This attractive species grows on limestone hills in Mexico up to more than 1000m alt. It can be solitary or form a crowded clump, the individual globose stems deeply ribbed with a strongly bluish green colouration and yellow spines. Long-lasting pale yellow bell-shaped flowers are produced during spring and summer. This species will tolerate light frost only.

Ferocactus hamatacanthus Mexican Fruit Cactus

This *Ferocactus* is one of the few species that will flower while still quite young. Occurring naturally in the USA (New Mexico and Texas) and northern Mexico, it is also one of the smaller species, growing to about 60 × 30cm. It has straggly or bristly spines that are sometimes twisted and often hooked at the tip, and funnel-shaped flowers (about 7cm across) that are yellow, often with a red throat. It adapts well to cultivation, tolerating light frost.

Ferocactus herrerae

A solitary cactus from Mexico that develops an egg-shaped deeply ribbed stem 1–2m tall and up to 45cm across. The broad central spines are hooked (very prominent in young plants) whereas the much thinner radial spines spread and often twist. Funnel-shaped yellow flowers about 6cm across (with a broad red stripe down the midline of each petal) are produced in abundance at the top of the stems in summer. These are followed by yellowish green fruit. This species tolerates light frost.

Ferocactus latispinus Devil's Tongue

A handsome species from Mexico that forms a single light green or greyish strongly ribbed globe-like stem to about 35 × 40cm. The central spine in each cluster is strongly hooked and much wider and thicker than the rest. Yellow, pink or rich purple funnel-shaped flowers appear in winter-spring. This species tolerates light frost.

Ferocactus macrodiscus Candy Cactus

A slow-growing collector's item from the central highlands of Mexico. This cactus has a single flattish dome-like stem 30–50cm across that is prominently and sharply ribbed, the ribs bearing groups of curved and spreading red or yellow spines. Decorative scaly buds at the top of the plant open to become lovely pink to purplish flowers (sometimes with a darker centre) in spring and summer. Protect from frost and water carefully.

Ferocactus pilosus Mexican Fire Barrel Cactus

A decorative slow-growing species that forms crowded clumps of domed cylinders, each growing more than 2m high and 50cm wide. Ornamented with rows of red spines that shine in the sun, this cactus also has showy yellow to red flowers (2.5cm across) in rings at the top, followed by yellow fruit. This cactus is an ideal specimen plant for a large container.

Ferocactus pottsii

Extending up to 1000m alt., this solitary Mexican species grows in deciduous forest. It forms a strongly ribbed ovoid to globe-like grey-green stem up to 1m high and 50cm across. Yellow to orange flowers, 3–3.5cm across, open widely in late summer–autumn, followed by yellow globe-like fruit. This species tolerates light frost.

Ferocactus robustus

This remarkable Mexican cactus, which looks best when grown in the ground, forms bright green mounds than can spread more than 4m wide and be up to 1m high. Each mound consists of hundreds of shiny globe-like stems 10–15cm across, each prominently ribbed and with widely spaced groups of spines. Yellow funnel-shaped flowers are followed by yellow fleshy fruit. This species can tolerate light frost.

Ferocactus schwarzii

Young plants of this Mexican cactus have numerous long yellowish spines that mask the ribs, whereas older plants have a deeply ribbed appearance with very few (sometimes none) short spines on the ridges. A solitary grower, it forms green ovoid stems and globes to 80 × 50cm. Prominent yellow flowers (4–5cm across) are produced in an apical ring, often providing a most attractive display. This species can tolerate light frost.

Paul Forster

Ferocactus schwarzii

Ferocactus pilosus in flower

Ferocactus pilosus

Ferocactus pottsii

Ferocactus macrodiscus

Ferocactus robustus

Paul Forster

Gymnocalycium baldianum

Michael Mathieson

Ferocactus macrodiscus

Gymnocalycium bruchii

Gymnocalycium eurypleurum

GYMNOCALYCIUM

Very popular with cactus enthusiasts, this genus of about 70 species from South America consists mainly of small to medium-sized plants, mostly with a solitary habit (some are clumping). They are often known as 'Chin Cacti' because of the chin-like protuberance on the ribs of some species. Colourful, funnel-shaped flowers, which arise near the growth apex in spring and summer, have distinctive buds covered with large scales. The diurnal flowers last for several days (sometimes 10–12 days). These cacti, which are mostly easy to grow, are excellent for the beginner. Best grown in a deep container (to accommodate the long taproot), they need excellent drainage, bright light (some in full sun, others need shelter from hot sun), good air movement and dry winter rest. Repot every two to three years using an acid mix. Some will tolerate cold, even frost, others need warmth. Increase by seed or careful division.

Gymnocalycium baldianum

Solitary or clustering, this Argentinian species is valued for its ease of growth and dark red or purplish red flowers. The somewhat flattened globose stems, 5–6cm across, have thin grey spines flattened against the stem surface. The flowers, which are about 4–5cm across, open sporadically in spring and summer. This species grows happily in full sun and tolerates light to moderate frost.

Gymnocalycium bruchii

Hardy to most frosts, this Argentinian species is relatively fast growing, eventually forming a dense clump with numerous small offsets. The dark green stems, which have thin curved spines, are crowned in spring by delicate pink to white flowers 3–4cm across.

Gymnocalycium eurypleurum

In nature this species is restricted to a small area of northern Paraguay where it grows in prickly scrub. It is solitary forming a globe-like growth 7–12cm across armed with clusters of curved brownish spines. Snowy white flowers (sometimes tinged pink) about 3cm across provide an attractive display from the top of the stem in spring.

Gymnocalycium gibbosum

A variable species that is widespread in the mountainous areas of Argentina. It is solitary with a ribbed globe-like bluish green growth 10–15cm across. Lovely white (sometimes pinkish) flowers 5–6cm across are produced in late spring and summer. This species will tolerate light frost.

Gymnocalycium gibbosum

Gymnocalycium horstii

Native to Brazil and possibly also occurring in adjacent countries, this slow-growing species produces offsets with age. The smooth bright green ball-like stems are deeply furrowed with broadly rounded ribs and well separated groups of spidery spines. White, pink or purplish flowers about 10cm across appear in the warmer months. This species will tolerate light to moderate frosts.

Gymnocalycium horstii

Gymnocalycium mihanovichii
Chin Cactus

Probably the most commonly grown species in the genus, this cactus, native to Paraguay, is extremely variable. Chin cactus plants can be solitary or produce offsets. The plants themselves have attractive reddish bands and white to greenish flowers, each 4–5cm long, open widely on sunny days. This easily grown species will tolerate frost. Many different colourful mutant cultivars, known as Moon Cacti or Lollypops, are also available. These cultivars, occurring in a range of colours including red, yellow, orange and purple, can be perpetuated only by grafting since they lack chlorophyll. Although a highly decorative novelty, these grafts can be short-lived. A bronze-coloured crested form of the species is also grown.

Ron Tunstall

Gymnocalycium mihanovichii rose-purple mutant

Gymnocalycium mihanovichii

Ron Tunstall

Gymnocalycium mihanovichii 'Hibotan'

Gymnocalycium paraguayense

Now reduced to great rarity in the wild, this Paraguayan species grows naturally in shallow soil over sheets of sandstone. In cultivation it grows well, produces offsets and flowers freely. The attractive flowers, each about 5cm across, are white with a ruby pink throat.

Gymnocalycium paraguayense

Gymnocalycium saglionis Giant Chin Cactus

Moderately large growing for the genus, this solitary species, native of northern Argentina, grows 10–15cm high and 20–30m across. It has numerous ribs with prominent rounded tubercles and curved spines. White or pink flowers 2–3cm across (sometimes with a darker throat) are produced at intervals over spring and summer, but only on larger plants. The small round fleshy fruit are red when ripe. This species will tolerate light frost.

Gymnocalycium schickendantzii

Native to northern Argentina, this species exhibits much variation in the density and length of its spines, with some plants densely spiny, others appearing almost spineless. It is a solitary species with a ribbed stem to about 10cm across. White, pink or reddish flowers 4–5cm across, with a long basal tube, are produced in spring and early summer.

Gymnocalycium stellatum

A slow-growing species from Argentina that mostly stays single, although it can produce offsets with age. Growing best in bright filtered light rather than full sun, it has globose ribbed stems and white to pink flowers with a darker throat. This species will tolerate light frost.

Paul Forster

Gymnocalycium saglionis

Gymnocalycium schikendantzii

Gymnocalycium stellatum

Haageocereus pacalaensis flowers

Haageocereus pacalaensis

Haageocereus versicolor

× *Haagespostoa* sp.

HAAGEOCEREUS

A genus of about 20 species of column-like to tree-like cacti (some have a sprawling habit) native to dry desert areas of Peru and Chile. The stems are very spiny and the tubular to funnel-shaped flowers arise near the stem apex. Few species are grown. The tall species are suitable for a large container or a dry garden in full sun. Some will tolerate cold (including frost), but not excessive rain. Increase by seed or stem cuttings.

Haageocereus pacalaensis

A clumping species from northern Peru with cylindrical stems to 1m tall covered with yellowish spines. White flowers 8–10cm long are produced in late spring–summer. This species will tolerate light frost.

Haageocereus versicolor

Native to Peru, this adaptable species has stems to 1.5m long that can sprawl with age. Covered with yellow to brown spines, in spring and summer they carry white flowers about 7cm across. This species will tolerate light frost.

× *HAAGESPOSTOA*

Three species from Peru that have arisen as a result of natural hybridisation between species of *Haageocereus* and *Espostoa*. Two of the species have also been placed in *Neobinghamia*. One easily grown undescribed species is available in Australia. Increase by stem cuttings.

× *Haagespostoa* sp.

A clumping species with deeply ribbed, spiny, column-like stems to 1m or more tall. Young parts are covered with reddish spines. Tufts of white hairs develop into hairy buds that open to tomato-red flowers 4–5cm across from spring to autumn. The flowers, which are open during the day, last for one to two days. This species will tolerate light frost.

LEUCHTENBERGIA

The single species in this genus is a very distinctive Mexican cactus with long, thin, somewhat leaf-like tubercles that are triangular in cross-section, and with unusual flattened papery spines arising from an apical areole. The showy diurnal flowers last for several days. Relatively easy to grow, this species needs depth for its taproot to develop and careful watering (too dry over summer and the tubercles brown off at the tips, too wet and the plants rot). Gritty, freely draining soil is recommended. It tolerates light to moderate frost. Increase by seed. This species can also be propagated from removed tubercles which are buried up to the areole in propagating mix.

***Leuchtenbergia principis* Agave Cactus**

Native to limestone areas in the Chihuahuan Desert of Mexico, this species grows best in a deep pot. Healthy plants have uniformly bluish green tubercles tipped with well-developed papery spines. Showy, fragrant, yellow, daisy-like flowers 6–10cm across, produced at intervals over the summer, are followed by smooth green fruit. Older plants form a short stem.

LOPHOPHORA

There are two or possibly three species in this well-studied genus of Mexican cacti which are better known for their medicinal and pharmacological properties rather than their horticultural qualities, because they contain the mind-altering alkaloid known as mescaline. Growing in limestone soils of the Chihuahuan Desert in Texas and Mexico, they form crowded clumps, sometimes mounds, of flattened spineless stems. The plants have a large taproot and their flowers have unusual anthers that curl over to release the pollen after being touched. The region where these cacti grow is subject to heavy summer rain and some of the plants can be underwater for long periods. Winters are dry and frosty. Despite their specialised habitat, these cacti are relatively easy to grow. They respond to hot temperatures and careful watering over summer (allow plants to dry between waterings). Overwatering can cause cracking and rotting. The plants must be kept dry in winter. Increase from seed and by careful division.

Leuchtenbergia principis

Paul Forster

Leuchtenbergia principis

Lophophora williamsii

Lophophora williamsii Peyote

This, the most commonly grown and variable species, has grey to bluish stems 5–10cm across adorned with prominent grooves. Pale pink (sometimes reddish) flowers are produced in summer. Flowering usually occurs in the wild after heavy rain and cultivated plants can be encouraged to flower by watering heavily in summer after a dry spell of two to three weeks. This species is often grafted. It will tolerate light frost.

MAMMILLARIA

Cherished by cacti devotees, this popular genus consists of about 250 species of dwarf to small solitary and clumping cacti that are valued for their symmetry, spine ornamentation (including wool) and attractive flowers, which can be produced in abundance over many months. Mainly from Mexico, but extending from south-western USA to South America, the genus includes many of the most commonly grown cacti. Globe-like to elongate cylindrical stems are covered with small nipple-like structures (called tubercles) carrying apical spines. The axils between the tubercles often contain hairs or bristles. Some species produce milky sap or latex from damaged areas. Increase in the clumping species is either by basal branching (offsets) or dichotomous division (forking – see photo of *M. muehlenpfordtii*). The flowers, which arise from axils between the tubercles, often appear in a ring on two-year-old growth (not the youngest apical areas). The fleshy fruit, mostly pink to red, are elongate to club-shaped and may still be present at next seasons flowering. Many of these decorative cacti are easily grown and are excellent for the beginner, but some are very difficult. The smaller types and more compact growers are best grown as container plants (often in shallow pots), whereas the larger ones can be planted out. These cacti, some of which are fast growers, need excellent drainage, bright light (some in full sun), good air movement and dry winter rest. Repot every two to three years. Some will tolerate cold, even frost, others need warmth. It should be mentioned here that some of these cacti exhibit considerable variation in growth morphology and cultivated plants can be difficult to identify accurately. Increase by seed or careful division.

Mammillaria albicoma

A slow-growing species from Mexico where it grows at 1400–1700m alt. A clumper, it eventually forms a flat-topped mound of crowded stems covered with long pale hair-like spines. Individual stems, 3–5cm diameter, are globose. Funnel-shaped greenish, cream or yellow flowers 1–1.5cm across open in spring. A variant with short spines is sometimes grown. This species will tolerate light frost.

Mammillaria albicoma

Mammillaria albilanata

Usually solitary, but occasionally clumping, this species has globe-like to small barrel-shaped stems (to 10cm tall and wide) that are covered with tightly appressed white spines. Short to long coarse white woolly hairs add greatly to the plant's decorative appeal. Pink to purplish or red funnel-shaped flowers are produced near the top in spring. This species, which will tolerate light frost and is easy to grow, can rot quickly from overwatering.

Tony Wood

Mammillaria albilanata

Mammillaria backebergiana

Easily grown, this Mexican species forms a slender cylinder 20–30cm high and 4–6cm across. The plants tend to lean with age and may eventually become prostrate, sometimes branching from the base to develop into an interesting leaning clump. Yellowish to brown spines clothe the stems and pink to red flowers arise in rings near the apex. Occurring in nature at about 1500m alt., this species will tolerate light frost.

Mammillaria bocasana Powder Puff Cactus

A variable species from Mexico where it grows in the mountains up to 2300m alt. Relatively fast growing, it forms crowded clumps or mounds, each stem covered with a mixture of bristles, soft hair-like spines and hooked spines which catch on clothing (in the wild they have also been known to trap small birds and animals). Funnel-shaped cream to pink flowers appear among the hair-like spines in spring and summer. This species will tolerate frost. An unusual crested form is sometimes available. Note the variation shown in the two photos.

Mammillaria backebergiana

Mammillaria bocasana

Pual Forster

Mammillaria bocasana in fruit

Mammillaria bombycina
Silken Pincushion

An easily grown Mexican species that can form clumps 50–80cm wide, with each stem covered with spreading white or red spines and wool. Hooked central spines catch effectively on clothing and skin. Funnel-shaped pink or white flowers are produced in circles near the top of the stems during spring. This species will tolerate frost. 'Bridal Ball' is a strongly offsetting variant of this popular species.

Mammillaria bombycina

Mammillaria bombycina 'Bridal Ball'

Mammillaria canelensis

Eventually offsetting to form a clump, this species, which occurs naturally in Chihuahua, Mexico growing at about 2000m alt., has flattish globose stems about 10cm across. Dense wool lines the axils and the tubercles carry curved needle-like spines. Flowers range in colour from yellow to pink and even occur in brownish tones. This easily grown species will tolerate light frost.

Mammillaria compressa Mother of Hundreds

A fast-growing clumper from Mexico than can spread to nearly 1m across. Cylindrical to club-shaped grey-green stems with white spines can form a dome to 25cm tall. Bell-shaped flowers, pink to red are produced freely in spring. This species, which can be grown in a dry garden, will tolerate frost. A form with extra long spines is often grown.

Michael Mathieson

Mammillaria canelensis

Tony Wood

Mammillaria compressa flowers

Mammillaria compressa

Mammillaria crinita

Fine hairs adorn the spines of this easily grown species, these hairs especially apparent on the appressed and spreading radial spines. Widely distributed in Mexico, this species grows in habitats at altitudes ranging from 1400 to 2300m. The globose stems form a tight cluster, each stem with white to yellow spines and white, yellowish or pale pink flowers. Although easy to grow, this species needs some protection from excessive hot sun.

Michael Mathieson

Mammillaria crinita

Mammillaria elongata

A popular clumper that forms compact clusters of slender cylindrical stems to 10cm long that are clothed with closely appressed non-prickly spines occurring in a range of colours from white to yellow or coppery bronze. Small pale yellow to pinkish funnel-shaped flowers are produced in spring and at intervals over summer. This easily grown species is best in a small pot that snugly accommodates the root system. It will tolerate light frost. Named cultivars are sometimes available, some resulting as hybrids with *M. microhelia*. A crested form is sometimes grown.

Mammillaria elongata

Mammillaria elongata

Pual Forster

Mammillaria flavicentra in habitat on cycad trunk

Tony Wood

Mammillaria formosa

Tony Wood

Mammillaria fraileana

Mammillaria flavicentra

In nature this species usually grows in the clefts and fissures of rocks but, as the photo shows, it has also been seen growing perched on the trunks of cycads. This cactus, which is usually solitary, has a neat cylindrical stem covered with yellow spines. Small pale pink to red flowers are produced from near the top of the plant in spring. A slow but steady grower, this species is from high alt. areas (1200–2500m) in Mexico.

Mammillaria formosa Owl Eyes

The stems of this variable Mexican species increase by forking, with each growth dividing down the middle. They can also develop basal offsets. This species is easy to grow and will eventually form a clump about 50cm across. Funnel-shaped pink or white flowers are produced in spring and sometimes again in summer. This species will tolerate light frost if kept dry.

Mammillaria fraileana

A slow grower that can be difficult to maintain. It needs very careful watering (underwater rather than overwater), acid mineral mix low in organic matter, good ventilation and a dry winter rest. The attractive flowers, 20–25mm across, are white or pink with a prominent starfish-like stigma.

Mammillaria geminispina Twin-spined Cactus

This Mexican species, which varies considerably in its clumping habit, woolliness and spination, forms clumps of short cylindrical stems, each with white wool and short to long white spines. It needs bright light to maintain the pristine appearance. Pink to red funnel-shaped flowers (sometimes with darker central bands) are produced in spring and autumn (although this species can be a shy flowerer). Frost damage can spoil the appearance of this species. A crested

Tony Wood

Mammillaria geminispina subsp. *leucocentra*

form is sometimes grown. The subsp. *leucocentra* (sometimes treated as a distinct species) is covered densely with white wool and has pure white spines.

Mammillaria hahniana subsp. *bravoae*

Mammillaria hahniana
Old Lady Cactus

A variable clumping species that is relatively easy to grow. The flattish globe-like stems are covered with pale spines and tufts of white bristly hairs (prominent at the apex). Some forms also have long hair-like spines. Small funnel-shaped pink to red flowers appear in a ring near the top of the plant in spring and sometimes also later in summer. The subsp. *bravoae* has different spination and very short hairs. *Mammillaria hahniana* will tolerate light frost. A crested form is sometimes grown as a graft.

Mammillaria geminispina subsp. *geminispina*

Paul Forster

Mammillaria hahniana subsp. *hahniana,* hairy variant

Tony Wood

Mammillaria hahniana subsp. *hahniana*

Michael Mathieson

Mammillaria humboldtii

Mammillaria humboldtii

Individual stems of this clumping Mexican species resemble a snowball. When viewed up close, the clusters of intensely white radiating spines can be seen to form a series of startling white starbursts over the whole of the stem surface. These spines, together with white wool and bristles in the axils of the tubercles, provide a nice backdrop to the bright purplish pink funnel-shaped flowers that appear in spring. Easily grown, this species will tolerate light frost.

Mammillaria hutchisoniana

One of a group of species that has cylindrical stems and large flowers with a prominent starfish-like stigma. The light green stems, to 15 × 5cm, have a long hooked spine that protrudes from a cluster of spreading radial spines. The flowers, to 3cm across, are pale pink with darker central bands. This slow-growing species, native to the Baja California Peninsula in Mexico, needs careful watering. The subsp. *louisae* has white to pale pink flowers with pink midveins.

Mammillaria karwinskiana Royal Cross

Commonly grown and valued for its ease of growth, this vigorous clumping species has conspicuous tufts of white bristles in the axils of the younger tubercles. These contrast with the dark green shortly cylindrical stems that grow to about 15cm tall and 7cm wide. Although it can take several years to flower, the cream to pink flowers with darker midveins in the petals are worth waiting for. It will tolerate light to moderate frost, even heavier if kept dry. The subsp. *nejapensis* lacks any central spines and has fewer radial spines (three to five) than in the typical form.

Mammillaria lindsayi

A slow growing species that offsets freely and eventually forms a large clump. It is native to Mexico where it grows in rock crevices at about 2000m alt. Individual stems are globose with dense woolly axils. Pale yellow to bright yellow flowers about 1cm across open in spring. This attractive species grows well in a pot. It will tolerate light frost.

Tony Wood

Mammillaria hutchisoniana subsp. *louisae*

Paul Forster

Mammillaria karwinskiana subsp. *nejapensis*

Michael Mathieson

Mammillaria lindsayi

Tony Wood

Mammillaria longiflora subsp. *stampferi*

Mammillaria longimamma

Paul Forster

Mammillaria longimamma clump

Mammillaria longiflora

Often sold in pots and labelled as *Krainzia longiflora*, this attractive little species (solitary or clustering) forms short cylindrical stems covered with radiating white spines and longer brown central spines. Bright pink flowers, each 20–30mm across, open widely on sunny spring days to provide an arresting display. The subsp. *stampferi* has short central spines (or none at all) and rose-pink flowers. This species is usually short-lived in cultivation.

Mammillaria longimamma Nipple Cactus

Previously placed in the genus *Dolichothele*, this easily grown Mexican species has stems to about 15cm across, each stem with bright green nipple-like tubercles tipped with radiating whitish spines. Bright yellow flowers appear in spring and summer. Initially solitary, the older plants branch to form a clump. This species will tolerate some frost.

Mammillaria magnifica

A clumping Mexican species that grows well either in a pot or in a sunny to partly shady position in the ground. Moderately fast growing, it develops cylindrical stems 30–40cm tall, well-armed with brownish spines and white axillary wool. Red or purplish flowers are produced from mid- to late summer and autumn. This species will tolerate some frost.

Mammillaria longiflora

Mammillaria magnifica

Mammillaria magnimamma Mexican Pincushion

A variable Mexican species that eventually develops into a slowly spreading ground-hugging clump. Stem colour ranges from greyish green to dark green, and the spines vary greatly in length and number. The flowers are mostly reddish but can be cream or purplish. Adaptable in cultivation, this species can be grown in a pot or in a sunny to partly shady position in the ground. This species will tolerate some frost.

Mammillaria marksiana

A commonly grown Mexican species that has bright green to yellowish green somewhat flattish stems (often yellowish in full sun) with short thin, needle-like spines and apical wool. Greenish to pale yellow flowers are produced mainly in late-winter-spring. Slow growing, it will eventually form clumps, the individual stems 10–20cm across. Tolerates light frost.

Mammillaria melanocentra

A solitary species which has somewhat flattened globe-like stems up to 12cm across. The tubercles have relatively long thin spines, the outer greyish white ones radiating around a longer central black spine. Whitish to bright pink flowers appear in summer–autumn. This Mexican species, which will tolerate light frost, benefits from repotting every two years.

Mammillaria microhelia

This easily grown species often develops a central column 10–15cm tall, surrounded by a basal ring of offsets. It is covered with clusters of radiating needle-like spines. Rings of cream, yellowish or pink flowers appear in late spring. A crested form is sometimes grown. This species, which occurs above 2000m alt. in Mexico, will tolerate light frost.

Mammillaria microhelia

Paul Forster

Mammillaria magnimamma

Mammillaria melanocentra

Mammillaria marksiana

Mammillaria muehlenpfordtii

Paul Forster

Mammillaria mystax

Tony Wood

Mammillaria mystax

Tony Wood

Mammillaria nunezii

Mammillaria nunezii

Paul Forster

Mammillaria obconella

Mammillaria muehlenpfordtii

Although often solitary, this decorative species can also form clumps by forking. The bluish to greyish globose stems, 10–15cm across, are covered with yellowish to brownish spines. Small red flowers appear in late spring and summer. Best in sun, this species is relatively fast growing. Native to highland areas in Mexico above 1700m alt., it will tolerate some frost.

Mammillaria mystax

Widely distributed in Mexico, this species grows in a range of habitats up to more than 2000m alt. It is usually solitary with the flattish globe-like stems covered with ribbed tubercles and stout overlapping brown spines. Attractive displays of lovely pink flowers are produced in spring. This species will tolerate light frost.

Mammillaria nunezii

Although often remaining as a single growth, older plants of this Mexican species can sometimes produce basal offsets and form a sparse clump with cylindrical stems 10–15cm tall. Bright pink funnel-shaped flowers about 15mm across produce an attractive display in late spring. Native to areas above 1000m alt, this species will tolerate light frost.

Mammillaria obconella

Treated by some authorities as a subspecies of *M. polythele*, this Mexican cactus, which occurs in mountainous areas above 1300m alt., is a clumper with blue-green shortly cylindrical stems 20–30cm tall and 10–15cm across. Yellowish radial spines, usually in fours, are arranged in the form of a cross. Pink to red flowers are produced during the summer months. This species will tolerate light frost.

Mammillaria parkinsonii Owl's-eye Pincushion

A clumping species from relatively high alt. (1200–2000m) in Mexico that branches by forking, eventually forming a mound-like clump up to 1m across. Individual stems are bluish green, the younger parts heavily ornamented with white wool and bristles. Thin spines (often curved) are variable in length. Pale yellow flowers 10–15mm across appear in summer. The most compact clumps develop in full sun. This species will tolerate some frost.

Mammillaria perezdelarosae

The stems of this decorative Mexican species, globose or forming a short cylinder, are densely clothed with white comb-like radial spines, the darker central spines protruding and often hooked. Greenish, whitish or very pale pink flowers (about 15mm across) are produced in spring from the upper parts of the stems. Occurring in nature at about 2000m alt. this species will tolerate light frost.

Mammillaria petrophila

Usually solitary, but sometimes offsetting sparsely, this Mexican species develops flattish globose stems 10–15cm across. Axils between the short conical tubercles are filled with dense white wool and stiff spines project from the tops of the tubercles. Greenish yellow to yellow flowers open during spring. Although somewhat slow, this species is easy to grow. It tolerates light frost.

Mammillaria plumosa Featherball Cactus

Paul Forster

Mammillaria plumosa

Few cacti are more friendly than this Mexican species, the stems of which are covered with white wool and soft feather-like spines. Rare in nature but common in cultivation, it branches freely to form densely crowded mounds 20–40cm across. Fragrant white or pinkish flowers are produced in winter-spring. Although relatively easy to grow, this species can rot quickly if overwatered or suffering from poor drainage as the root system is weak. It can also die if allowed to become too dry at any time of the year. For best appearance avoid wetting the plant when watering.

Mammillaria parkinsonii

Tony Wood

Mammillaria perezdelarosae

Mammillaria petrophila

Mammillaria plumosa flowers

Paul Forster

Mammillaria polyedra

Mammillaria pseudoperbella

Mammillaria polyedra

Young parts of the globose stems of this clumping Mexican species appear as if snow-capped, an appearance created by the axillary tufts of white wool. The stems themselves are dark green with spreading needle-like spines. Pale pink to bright pink flowers are produced in late spring and summer. Occurring at about 1500m alt. in nature, this species will tolerate some frost.

Mammillaria pseudoperbella

Native to mountainous areas of Mexico above 1500m alt., this easy-to-grow, solitary species starts life as a globe and eventually grows into a cylinder about 20 × 6cm. The plant is covered with crowded groups of white radiating spines and in spring, pink funnel-shaped flowers appear, each recurved petal with a darker central stripe.

Mammillaria rhodantha Rainbow Pincushion

This species, widely distributed in a range of habitats in Mexico, exhibits considerable variation, with six subspecies recognised. Plants can be solitary or clump via forking or the production of basal offsets. Stem shape ranges from globose to cylindrical and pink to purplish flowers appear over most of the year especially the warmer months. Moderately easy to grow, this species will tolerate light frost. The subsp. *pringlei* has paler stems with yellow radial spines.

Mammillaria rhodantha subsp. *pringlei*

Mammillaria schiedeana

A compact clumping species the stems of which are completely covered with closely appressed whitish to yellow, finely hairy, multi-armed spines that resemble the pappus of a daisy flower. White flowers 10–15mm across are produced in summer and autumn, followed by long red fruit. This species, which has a fleshy taproot and can be tricky to grow, does best in a mix that includes limestone chips. It occurs at up to 5000m alt. in the mountains of Mexico. The subsp. *dumetorum* has stiffly rigid spines (fewer than in the typical subsp.) and subsp. *giselae* has no axillary hairs and even less spines that are flexible rather than rigid.

Mammillaria schumannii Schumann's Pincushion

Unusual within this genus, this species has large pink flowers and dryish fruit that break off near the base when ripe. It clumps freely, the grey-green to blue-green globose or cylindrical stems (pink to purplish in bright light) bearing prominent pale-coloured radial spines. Lovely pink to purplish flowers, which can be up to 4cm across, make this species popular with collectors, although it can be difficult to grow. Protect from frost.

Mammillaria sheldonii Sheldon's Pincushion

A slow grower that must be watered carefully because of its small root system. It needs an acid mineral mix low in organic matter, good ventilation and a dry winter rest. The attractive funnel-shaped flowers range from nearly white to purplish pink. This species tolerates light frosts.

Mammillaria sphacelata

A clumping species that can form mounds of slender cylindrical stems 30–50cm across. Pink to purple flowers, that often do not open widely, are produced near the top of the stems in spring. This species will tolerate light frost. The subsp. *viperina* has slender erect to sprawling snake-like stems about 2cm thick.

Michael Mathieson

Mammillaria schiedeana subsp. *dumetorum*

Michael Mathieson

Mammillaria schiedeana subsp. *giselae*

Mammillaria schiedeana subsp. *schiedeana*

Tony Wood

Mammillaria schumannii

Tony Wood

Mammillaria sheldonii

Tony Wood

Mammillaria sphacelata subsp. *viperina*

Michael Mathieson

Mammillaria surculosa

Mammillaria spinosissima 'Un Pico'

Mammillaria vetula subsp. *gracilis*

Mammillaria spinosissima

Usually solitary, this popular Mexican species develops as a dark blue-green slender cylinder 20–30cm tall, ornamented with prominent groups of pale bristle-like spines. Showy purplish-red flowers are produced in rings. The cultivar 'Un Pico' is a mutant form of very distinctive appearance since each tubercle only produces a single long spine (spineless tubercles are also present). Solitary or clumping, it grows to about 30cm tall and also produces colourful floral displays. A crested form of the mutant is also grown. *Mammillaria spinosissima* and its cultivars will tolerate light to moderate frost.

Mammillaria supertexta

Sometimes shaped like a small barrel, the globose tocylindrical stems of this attractive Mexican species are covered with white hairs and white spines closely appressed to the surface. Usually clumping with age, it produces rings of small bright pink to purplish flowers from near the top of the stems. Protect from frost.

Mammillaria surculosa

Originally included in the genus *Dolichothele*, this Mexican species, which grows at about 1000m alt., has a sturdy taproot and clustering bright green stems adorned with prominent tubercles. Widely opening pale yellow fragrant flowers appear near the top of each stem in spring. Well-grown plants produce an attractive floral display. This species will tolerate light frost.

Paul Forster

Mammillaria supertexta in habitat

Mammillaria vetula Thimble Cactus

Snowy white from the dense covering of spines, this popular fast-growing Mexican species branches freely to form a clump. Small, cream to yellowish tubular flowers appear at intervals at almost any time of the year. This species is easily propagated from stems that break off readily. The subsp. *gracilis* has fewer spines in each cluster (usually no central spines) and smaller flowers.

Mammillaria zeilmanniana Rose Pincushion Cactus

In nature this lovely, but rare Mexican species grows in a narrow canyon close to flowing water in shade and constant humidity. Although from a specialised habitat, it adapts well to cultivation, growing quickly and clumping freely. The large bright pink flowers (rarely white) provide an attractive display at intervals in spring and summer. Recent studies link this species with *M. crinita*.

MATUCANA

A genus of seventeen to nineteen species from the Andes mountains in Peru, often growing at high elevations (2000–4000m alt.). They are low-growing solitary or clumping cacti with round to cylindrical stems and large upright colourful often zygomorphic flowers (red, pink, orange, yellow) that open during the day. Several species are pollinated in the wild by hummingbirds. These cacti can also be recognised by their distinctive juicy fruit that open by three vertical slits.

These cacti are relatively easy to grow but some can be slow. Sparsely spiny species need bright but diffuse light, densely spiny species will tolerate sun. Water freely over summer, less so in autumn and spring; keep dry over winter. Some species will tolerate light frost, others benefit from protection. Species such as *M. oreodoxa* have sparsely spiny soft growth that is easily damaged by pests and careless handling. Florally these cacti are rewarding, producing several flushes of flowers during spring and summer (sometimes all year). Repot every two to three years. Increase by seed.

Matucana aureiflora

The lovely bright yellow flowers of this popular species remain open for several days and are produced in flushes at intervals during spring and summer. They crown a single flattened globular stem 10–12cm diameter. that is bright green and shiny with well spaced clusters of spidery spines. This species, which needs a deep pot to accomodate its taproot, may be scarred if exposed to frost.

Matucana haynei

A variable species consisting of four subspecies ranging in height from 10–30cm tall. Becoming cylindrical with age, the stems, which can be sparsely or densely spiny, eventually lean or fall. Conspicuous red to purplish flowers provide intermittent eye-catching displays over summer. It will tolerate light frost.

Mammillaria zeilmanniana

Tony Wood

Matucana aureiflora

Paul Forster

Matucana haynei flowers

Matucana haynei

Matucana weberbaueri

This species has well-developed tubercles and long, sharp, needle-like spines. Typically the flowers are pale yellow to lemon yellow but an orange-flowered form (sometimes designated as var. *flammeus*) is often grown.

MELOCACTUS

There are about 33 species of these intriguing solitary cacti (from Central America, South America and the Caribbean), all of which exhibit distinct juvenile and adult growth phases. Young (non-reproductive) plants are simple and globe-like or melon-shaped (resembling many other cactus genera); however, mature plants develop a distinctive cap (known as a cephalium) that consists of wool and bristles arising from a dense mass of areoles. Once the cephalium appears, the main plant no longer increases in size but the cephalium grows steadily over many years producing flowers and fruit from among the areoles. The short-lived flowers, which are relatively inconspicuous, open in the afternoon or evening. They are followed by conspicuous pink, red or white tubular fruit.

Melocactus can be tricky to grow well. They are slow growing and very prone to rot, therefore needing a shallow container and excellent drainage. They also need warmth and it is wise to protect all species from severe winter cold, especially frost. Species that originate in the tropics are very cold sensitive. Water regularly in summer and sufficiently in winter to prevent the plants becoming excessively dry. Repot infrequently. Increase by seed.

Melocactus bahiensis Turk's Cap Cactus

One of the easier species to grow, this Brazilian plant develops a green stem to about 20cm across and a brown woolly cephalium that eventually reaches about 5cm tall. Pinkish flowers are followed by pink to red fruit. This species will tolerate light frost.

Melocactus curvispinus

A widely distributed species that extends from Mexico and the Caribbean region to Colombia and Venezuela. In some areas it grows in mountainous parts up to 1500m alt. The plants, which are often cylindrical, have a relatively short cephalium, magenta flowers and pink to red club-shaped fruit. This species will not tolerate frost.

Tony Wood

Matucana weberbaueri

Tony Wood

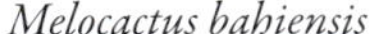

Melocactus bahiensis

Melocactus curvispinus

Melocactus matanzanus

Tony Wood

Micranthocereus polyanthus

Melocactus matanzanus

A small species growing 10–12cm tall with a relatively short cephalium that consists of a mixture of rusty red bristles and white wool. Dark red to scarlet flowers are followed by large pink fruit. This adaptable species will grow well in quite shady conditions.

MICRANTHOCEREUS

A genus of nine species of medium sized to large cacti from Brazil. Mostly clumping (sometimes solitary), they have prominently ribbed, densely spiny columnar stems. Tubular flowers (often small), which appear in crowded clusters in a loose woolly or spiny cephalium, are followed by small fleshy fruit. Although sometimes grown in a pot, these cacti need room to reach their potential and are best planted out. They need sun or partial shade, excellent drainage, free air movement and dry winter rest. Increase by seed or stem cuttings.

Micranthocereus polyanthus

Often growing naturally in the shelter of shrubs, this clumping species has slender, erect to sprawling stems to about 1m tall. The stems, which are covered with white wool and yellow spines, produce numerous small flowers in crowded clumps near the top. Attractive when well grown, this species needs protection from frost.

MYRTILLOCACTUS

A genus of four species of shrubby to tree-like cacti found naturally in Mexico and Guatemala. Sometimes locally abundant they can dominate the vegetation, even forming their own forests. The plants branch freely to form crowded clumps of spiny cylindrical stems. The diurnal flowers, which are small for the size of the plant, often arise in clusters. These large cacti are important to the local people for their edible flowers and berry-like fruit that are very sweet when ripe.

Excellent cacti for the landscape or a large container, these plants need ample room to develop fully. They need full sun, excellent drainage, free air movement and dry winter rest. Light frosts are generally tolerated but heavy frost can cause stem splitting, scarring and plant death. Increase by seed or stem cuttings in summer (keep dry for best root formation).

Myrtillocactus cochal

This species forms a freely branching clump to 2m or more tall, spreading even more widely. The ribbed stems, which are armed with black spines, curve upwards and form an impenetrable clump. Greenish to whitish flowers about 1cm across, are followed by red edible fruit.

Myrtillocactus cochal

Myrtillocactus geometrizans Bilberry Cactus

In nature (Mexico) this bushy species often forms dominant stands in shrubland. Growing 3–4m tall, it forms an impenetrable mass of blue-green, spiny, club-shaped stems. Small white flowers, produced at intervals over much of the year, are followed by sweet-tasting dark purple berry-like fruit.

Myrtillocactus schenckii Garambullo Cactus

A tree-like cactus that grows more that 3m tall with upright, deeply ribbed, dark green stems lined with rows of blackish spines. Whitish flowers 3–4cm across are followed by sweet, red, berry-like fruit about 15mm across.

NEOBUXBAUMIA

There are nine species in this genus of large Mexican columnar cacti, some with a candelabra-like habit. In some parts of southern Mexico they dominate the landscape, forming remarkable forests. All species are sturdy cacti with a well-developed trunk and upright ribbed stems and branches (some remain unbranched). Relatively small, often pale-coloured nocturnal flowers are followed by dryish spiny fruit that split when ripe.

Uncommonly grown, these large cacti require plenty of room to reach their potential. Well suited to the semi-arid climates of inland towns, they need full sun, excellent drainage, free air movement and dry winter rest. Protect from heavy frost. Increase by seed or stem cuttings.

Neobuxbaumia polylopha Cone Cactus

An imposing species that can grow 8–10m tall with sturdy stems 40–50cm thick. The stems, which are prominently ribbed (the ribs are sometimes wavy), are well armed with sharp reddish spines. Fleshy red bell-shaped flowers about 3.5cm across are produced on the upper parts of the stems from spring to autumn.

Neobuxbaumia scoparia

A very large cactus that produces numerous moderately slender stems (10–15cm across) arising from a single trunk. Growing in excess of 10m tall, a mature plant is an impressive specimen indeed. Young spines on the growing tips are reddish or yellowish and reddish bell-shaped flowers are produced on the upper parts of the stems in summer.

Myrtillocactus geometrizans

Myrtillocactus geometrizans, flower and developing fruit

Myrtillocactus schenckii with threading stems of *Corryocactus melanotrichus*

Neobuxbaumia polylopha

Neobuxbaumia scoparia

NEORAIMONDIA

Both species in this genus are large cacti with a tree-like or candelabra-like growth and thick, strongly ribbed columnar stems. Short peg-like structures (modified areoles) protrude from the ribs. Diurnal flowers arise from these long-lived structures on the upper parts of the stems (each can produce flowers over many years). These cacti can be grown in a pot when small but must be repotted frequently and eventually planted out to achieve maturity. Slow growing, they need full sun, good drainage, good ventilation and winter dryness. Protect from frost. Increase by seed or stem cuttings.

Neoraimondia arequipensis

Neoraimondia arequipensis

A robust cactus that branches from the base to form a shrubby clump that can reach 8–10m tall. Individual stems 30–40cm thick have protruding peg-like areoles 3–5cm long. Small greenish white to reddish flowers develop from these areoles in summer. Purple spiny fruit follow the flowers.

OPUNTIA

A large genus of distinctive cacti consisting of 180–200 species distributed naturally from Canada to South America, including the Caribbean region and the Galápagos Islands. They range from prostrate plants to tree-like species growing 20–30m tall. These cacti have jointed stems consisting of flattened paddle-like segments (termed cladodes) that can photosynthesise and take the place of leaves. Normal spines present on the cladodes are supplemented by tufts of tiny barbed spines termed glochids. Glochids, which are readily detached from the plant, penetrate skin causing irritation and can also become airborne when the plants are handled. Colourful flowers on the cladode margins are followed by large fleshy fruit that are edible when ripe.

Opuntia ficus-indica, ripe fruit

Although highly decorative and easy to grow, these cacti are mostly avoided by hobbyists because of their ability to spread and become naturalised as weeds (see page 28). In fact it is illegal to grow them in some Australian states and some cactus societies also ban them from display in shows. Mostly easy to grow, they need sun, excellent drainage and an open position. Some will tolerate winter rainfall and many tolerate frost. Increase by seed or stem segments.

Opuntia ficus-indica Indian Fig

Although this cactus probably originated in Mexico, it is so widely cultivated for its edible fruit that its origins are now lost. The plants, which can grow 1–3m tall (or more) are tree-like with a distinctive trunk and flattened green segments. The spines are generally small and the glochids shed early as the pads mature. Self-pollinating red or yellow flowers are followed by large fig-like fruit that ripen orange-red.

Opuntia microdasys Bunny Ear Cactus

This commonly grown Mexican species lacks spines but the pads are covered with tufts of readily dislodged glochids. These are mainly yellow or brown but a variant with white glochids (forma *albata*) is also grown. Although it can reach 1m tall,

Opuntia microdasys, white spined variant

Opuntia microdasys

this cactus is more usually seen as a smaller plant growing in the confines of a container.

Opuntia santa-rita

Opuntia santa-rita Purple Prickly Pear

A highly decorative species with purplish green to violet-purple pads and colourful yellow flowers (each about 1cm across), often with a bright red central patch. Easily grown, this North American/Mexican species attains best colouration in full sun. It grows 1–2m tall and tolerates light to moderate frost.

OREOCEREUS

A small genus of nine species from high alt. (above 3000m) in the Andes of Peru, Chile, Bolivia and Argentina. They are clumping cacti with cylindrical stems ranging from prostrate to 2–3m tall columns. The stems and spines are covered with woolly hair. Tubular to funnel-shaped flowers arise near the stem tips in summer (only on older plants). Well suited to temperate regions, these cold-hardy cacti grow well in a container or dry garden. They need full sun (some prefer protection from very hot summer sun), good air movement and dry winter rest. Increase by seed or stem cuttings.

Oreocereus celsianus, flowers

Oreocereus celsianus

Oreocereus doelzianus var. *doelzianus*

Oreocereus doelzianus var. *sericatus*, flowers

Oreocereus doelzianus var. *sericatus*

Oreocereus celsianus Old Man of the Andes

This clumping species has sturdy green stems 1–2m tall and 10–12cm wide, covered with brownish spines and shaggy hairs. Unusual purplish tubular flowers 8–9cm long are carried on the tips of taller stems. Generally slow growing, but reliable, this variable species occurs in Bolivia, Peru and Argentina.

Oreocereus doelzianus Old Man of the Andes

Native to Peru, this cactus branches freely to form an open clump of straggly stems to 1m tall. In the typical form the stems are bright green with white areoles and hairs; however, in subsp. *sericatus* the stems are completely covered by fluffy white hairs. Bright red flowers 8–10cm long are produced in summer and autumn.

Oreocereus pseudofossulatus Old Man of the Mountains

Originating at high alt., this Bolivian species forms clumps to 2m tall, each stem covered with white to grey hair. Protruding through the hairs are sturdy yellowish spines. Pink to brownish tubular flowers 8–10cm long are produced from near the stem apex during spring and summer (sometimes also winter).

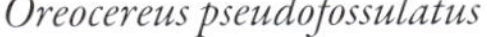

Oreocereus pseudofossulatus

Oreocereus pseudofossulatus flowers

Oreocereus trollii Old Man of the Mountains

An attractive, but slow-growing species from the mountains in Bolivia and Argentina. It forms clumps of densely woolly stems to 50cm tall, the stems sometimes prostrate. Yellowish brown spines protrude from the hairs and pink to red flowers about 4cm long appear in summer.

ORTEGOCACTUS

The single species in this genus is a novelty from Mexico. It can be difficult to grow successfully and is often grafted. It needs excellent drainage and is best in pot containing gritty mix. Water carefully at all times; keep dry in winter.

Ortegocactus macdougallii

This is a slow-growing, clumping species with small pale green to grey-green stems 3–4cm across adorned with plump tubercles and clumps of dark spines. Bright yellow funnel-shaped flowers 2.5–3cm across open during the day in spring and summer. This species will tolerate light frost.

PACHYCEREUS

A small genus of about twelve species distributed in south-western USA and Central America. Large, imposing cacti with a tree-like habit, they often have the erect shallowly ribbed stems arranged like a candelabra. The short nocturnal flowers are followed by fairly large fruit densely covered with wool and bristles. Mostly suited for planting out (especially in areas with a semi-arid climate), these large cacti need sun, good ventilation and dry winter rest. Frost tolerance is variable. Increase by seed and stem cuttings.

Pachycereus hollianus Baboso

This species is sometimes planted as a living fence in its native country of Mexico. It branches freely to form a crowded clump, the well-armed, pale green stems growing 3–5m tall. Tubular white flowers about 3.5cm across open widely on summer days, the floral tubes covered with small scales, wool and spine-like hairs. Ovoid purple fruit have a similar covering. This species will tolerate light frost.

Oreocereus trollii flowers

Oreocereus trollii

Ortegocactus macdougallii

Pachycereus hollianus

Pachycereus marginatus

Pachycereus pecten-aboriginum, buds and young fruit

Pachycereus pecten-aboriginum

Pachycereus schottii

Pachycereus marginatus Organ Cactus

In Mexico, this cactus, which can reach 3–5m tall, is frequently planted as a living fence or barrier. It has bright green columnar stems 10–20cm across with rows of short yellowish spines. Pink to red funnel-shaped flowers, produced in spring and summer, are followed by globose spiny/woolly fruit. This slow growing species will tolerate light frost.

Pachycereus pecten-aboriginum Hairbrush Cactus, Indian Comb

The unusual common name of this cactus comes from the fruit that are covered with yellow wool and stiff bristles to 6cm long. Dry fruit were used as a comb by the local Mexican people where it occurs naturally. With ribbed columnar stems growing 6–8m tall from a well defined trunk, this cactus is suitable only for planting out in a position with enough space for it to reach its potential. White flowers are 6–7cm long. Flowering habits vary with the climate of the area where the species grows. Populations in the tropics flower during the night, closing in the day (these are bat-pollinated), whereas in those from colder climates, the flowers remain open during the day (pollinated by both bats and hummingbirds). A crested form is sometimes grown as a novelty. This cactus needs protection from frost.

Pachycereus schottii Whisker Cactus

Occurring naturally in Arizona in south-western USA and north-western Mexico, this unusual species is readily recognised by the long flexible spines which develop in brush-like masses (termed pseudocephalia) towards the apex of mature stems. Growing 2–3m tall, it develops a multi-stemmed clump of pale green prominently ribbed columnar stems 8–10cm across. White to pink flowers 2.5–3cm diameter. develop among the 'whiskers', opening on summer nights. A monstrose form is also grown. This species will tolerate light frost.

Pachycereus weberi Candelabro, Cardón

A massive cactus from Mexico which can reach in excess of 10m tall. Because of its branching habit the plants can also spread a fair distance, and cultivated plants need ample room to develop fully. The stems are blue-green with blunt ribs and cream to yellowish flowers open at night. The reddish purple fruit contain edible flesh. Best in semi-arid climates, this species will tolerate light frost.

PARODIA

A genus of about 66 species of cacti from several countries in South America. In recent times a number of other cactus genera have been included in *Parodia*, notably species of *Notocactus* which are popular with enthusiasts as they are generally easy to grow and tolerant of winter frosts. Mostly with showy spines and colorful bell-shaped or funnel-shaped flowers that arise among wool near the top of the plant, these cacti range from small globose plants to columns about 1m tall. The diurnal flowers often last for several days. Some species are solitary, others form clumps. Best grown in a container, these cacti, most of which are slow growers, need excellent drainage, bright light (some in full sun), good air movement and dry winter rest. Some will tolerate cold, even frost, others need warmth. Increase by seed or careful division.

***Parodia chrysacanthion* Golden Powder Puff**

A solitary species from Argentina that develops a cylindrical stem to 20cm tall and 10cm wide. Clusters of long yellow bristle-like spines cover the stem surface and in spring, golden yellow flowers are produced from the stem apex, the flowers often subtebded by tufts of spines. This easily grown species will tolerate light to moderate frost.

Parodia comarapana

An easily grown cold-hardy species from high alt. in Bolivia. The plants, which slowly form clumps, have flattish bright green globe-like stems with thin spines and showy yellow to orange flowers in spring and summer. A commonly grown variant (sold as *P. mairanana*) has attractive orange to red flowers.

Paul Forster

Pachycereus weberi buds and flowers

Paul Forster

Pachycereus weberi

Michael Mathieson

Parodia chrysacanthion

Tony Wood

Parodia comarapana

Parodia concinna Sun Cup

The common name of this cactus arises from the bright yellow, shiny, cupped flowers that open freely on sunny days. Occurring naturally in Brazil and Uruguay, this easily grown species will tolerate frost if kept dry in winter. The plants, which are solitary, form a flattish globe-like growth to about 10cm across.

Parodia erubescens

Native to Uruguay, this solitary species develops into a ball-like growth 10–12cm across covered with stiff reddish spines. Attractive creamy yellow to lemony yellow flowers 4–4.5cm across open widely on sunny spring days.

Parodia concinna

Parodia fusca

A solitary Brazilian species that forms a globe-like stem 6–7cm across, with many wavy ribs and white wool prominent on the young areoles. Plump woolly buds open on sunny days into showy pale yellow flowers 25–30mm across.

Parodia haselbergii Scarlet Ball Cactus

The whole plant of this Brazilian cactus, usually a single globe-like ball 6–8cm across, is silvery grey to grey green from a dense covering of spines. The plants, which have numerous ribs arranged in a spiral, produce lovely orange to bright red flowers that open widely on warm spring and summer days. Care must be taken not to overwater this species.

Parodia horstii

Useful for its propensity to flower at any time of the year (even winter), this Brazilian cactus (solitary or clumping) is suitable for a pot or the garden. Easily grown, this sun-loving species will tolerate light to moderate frost without drawback. Commonly the flowers are orange to reddish, but purple-flowered plants are prized by collectors.

Parodia erubescens

Parodia horstii

Parodia haselbergii

Parodia fusca

Parodia leninghausii Yellow Tower

Commonly seen in cactus collections, this Brazilian species has also been successfully grown as a houseplant on brightly lit windowsills. Usually clumping, although sometimes remaining solitary, it forms column-like stems to about 1m tall. The stems, which are covered with long yellow to brown soft spines, carry groups of lemon yellow flowers (each 5–6cm across) in spring, summer and autumn. Easily grown, this species will tolerate frost if kept dry in winter. A colourful crested form is also grown.

Parodia leninghausii

Parodia magnifica
Golden Crown

Magnificent is a suitable description for a large-flowering plant of this Brazilian cactus. Solitary or clump-forming, it develops large globe-like stems 10–15cm across, each dark green stem deeply ribbed and adorned with clusters of soft bristle-like yellow spines. Clusters of shiny bright yellow flowers crown each stem at intervals over summer and autumn in impressive displays. This easily grown species (pot or dry garden) will tolerate frost if kept dry in winter. A strongly clumping form with whitish spines is sometimes segregated as var. *caespitosa*.

Parodia leninghausii in flower

Parodia magnifica var. *caespitosa*

Parodia ottonis

Widely distributed in Brazil, Paraguay and Uruguay, this species, which exhibits a high degree of variation, offers considerable scope for the collector. Mostly easy to grow, it forms clumps of globe-like stems 8–12cm across. The reddish-brown spines are relatively sparse on the ribs and yellow flowers (sometimes orange or reddish) open widely in spring and summer.

Parodia schumanniana

A solitary species from Paraguay, Argentina and Brazil that grows on exposed rocky hills. The plants form ribbed cylindrical stems or barrels to 1.8m tall and 30cm across, with relatively long bristle-like spines arising from the areoles. Cream, lemon or bright yellow flowers are produced in groups from the top of the growth. The subsp. *claviceps*, from Brazil, is smaller than the typical subspecies growing only 30–50cm tall.

Parodia scopa Silver Ball Cactus

A popular cactus valued for its silvery-white woolly stems and free-flowering habit. Native to Paraguay, Uruguay and Brazil, it can be solitary or clumping with globe-like or cylindrical stems to 50cm tall and 10cm across. Cream to yellow flowers 3–4.5cm across are produced at intervals over summer. An attractive crested form is also available. This is often seen grafted onto a tall rootstock, but can also be successfully grown on its own roots.

Parodia turecekiana

This cactus grows best in bright filtered light rather than full sun. Native to Argentina and Uruguay, the plants form a solitary globe-like growth 10–15cm across that is strongly ribbed and adorned with pale flattish spines. Shiny yellow flowers with a contrasting purple stigma appear over summer.

Tony Wood

Parodia scopa

Parodia magnifica

Parodia ottonis

Tony Wood

Parodia schumanniana subsp. *claviceps*

Parodia werneri Purple Crown

Easily grown and popular for its displays of mauve to purple flowers (rarely white), this Brazilian species can be solitary or clumping. It grows best in bright filtered light as plants can burn in excessive sun. When well grown the whole crown of the plant is covered with crowded flowers, each flower 4–4.5cm across, in a colourful display.

PELECYPHORA

Both species of this Mexican genus are small cacti from mountainous areas. They are solitary or clumping with globe-like stems that barely emerge above soil level. They have flattened tubercles and colourful diurnal flowers produced near the growth apex. These slow growing cold-hardy cacti grow well in a container. They need bright light, good ventilation and dry winter rest. Increase by seed or division.

Pelecyphora strobiliformis Pinecone Cactus

This cactus, which has a thick taproot, forms small globe-like stems less than 8cm across. Overlapping scale-like tubercles, with woolly margins and spiny tips cover the stems. Lovely pink to magenta flowers about 3cm across are produced in spring and summer.

PENIOCEREUS

This genus of eighteen species includes some unusual cacti with fleshy or tuberous roots that allow the plants to survive long dry periods. They also have slender stick-like stems that clamber through adjacent shrubs. Surprisingly they produce lovely flowers, many white and fragrant, some only opening during the night. These fast-growing cacti demand excellent drainage and resent high humidity. They are best grown in a container (including hanging baskets) where they can be easily moved to a suitable position, or in a dry garden against a north-facing wall. The slender sprawling to clambering stems may need staking or training through a shrub. They grow best in a sunny position with good air movement. Some species will tolerate very light frost. Although tolerant of dryness, these plants respond well to summer watering. Increase by seed, division and stem cuttings.

Parodia werneri

Parodia turecekiana

Tony Wood

Pelecyphora strobiliformis

Peniocereus serpentinus Snake Cactus

Native to southern Mexico, this intriguing cactus has tuberous roots and slender stems (3–5cm thick) that can grow 2–3m long. Deliciously fragrant, white (delicate pinkish outer segments), funnel-shaped flowers, each 20–25cm long and 12–15cm wide, open sporadically on warm nights from spring to autumn, finishing the next morning. The tall thin stems are easily broken by strong wind. An attractive narrowly crested form is sometimes grown as a graft.

PILOSOCEREUS

An interesting genus of 36 species of columnar cacti distributed from Mexico to Colombia. Characterised by having prominent woolly tufts near the stem tips through which the flowers arise, the genus includes a number of decorative species with grey to bluish stems. Some branch freely to form tree-like clumps. The unusual and sometimes smelly, fleshy flowers open at night, sometimes lasting the next morning. Best appearance is attained in a sunny airy position. Frost is best avoided. Increase by seed and stem cuttings.

Pilosocereus glauchocrous Blueboy

Although growing 3–5m tall, this Brazilian cactus usually forms a sparse clump with the blue to blue-green stems often leaning to one side. The prominent ribs carry clusters of yellow spines that become grey with age, and white woolly hairs. Pink to purplish buds open to pinkish tubular flowers with numerous stamens. This lovely species, which is best in full sun, should be kept completely dry over winter and sheltered from all but light frost.

Pilosocereus leucocephalus Woolly Torch Cactus

Young plants of this Central American cactus have columnar stems to 3m tall, but older plants can reach 4–5m after developing a trunk that supports its branching stems. Attractive variants with powdery blue stems are much sought after by collectors. The stems of mature plants are topped with clusters of silky white hairs through which the tubular white to pink flowers appear in spring and summer. Tolerates light frost only but must be dry over winter.

Peniocereus serpentinus, clump

Peniocereus serpentinus

Pilosocereus glaucochrous

Pilosocereus leucocephalus

Pilosocereus magnificus

Pilosocereus pachycladus

Polaskia chichipe, flower

Polaskia chichipe, young plant

Pilosocereus magnificus Blue Torch Cactus

Native to Brazil, this lovely species has waxy blue stems with clusters of yellow bristly spines along the ribs. Generally slow growing, it forms clumps 2–3m tall, sometimes more in nature. Unusual cream to brownish flowers with reflexed segments are produced from the stem tips from spring to autumn. This lovely species, which is best in full sun, should be kept completely dry over winter and sheltered from frost.

Pilosocereus pachycladus Facheiro

Widely distributed in north-eastern Brazil, this species has attractive blue to blue-green stems to 5m tall or more. Young spines are yellow, fading with age. Flower-bearing areoles carry dense tufts of white wool through which emerge dark-colored scaly buds that open in spring to white flowers about 4–5cm diameter. The flowers, which open at night, have an unusual smell resembling sour milk. Best colour is achieved in full sun. Protect from frost.

POLASKIA

This genus consists of two species of tree-like cacti from southern Mexico. The stems of large specimens branch repeatedly to form a canopy well above ground. Both species are ideal cacti for the landscape or a large container. They need full sun, free air movement and dry winter rest. Frost is best avoided. Increase by seed and stem cuttings.

Polaskia chichipe

In Mexico this large cactus is sometimes planted for the dark red fruit which are tasty when ripe. Plants can reach 3–4m tall, with a trunk-like main stem and spreading arm-like branches towards the apex. Cream to greenish flowers 3–4cm across open at night. This species will tolerate light frost only.

RAUHOCEREUS

The single species in this genus forms thickets in mountainous valleys of northern Peru. It can be grown in a pot or dry garden, preferring a sunny position. It needs good drainage, dry winter rest and summer watering. Increase by seed, division and stem cuttings.

Rauhocereus riosaniensis

Although the column-like stems of this cactus can reach 2–3m tall, it is generally very slow growing. It branches from the base to form a clump. White flowers 5–6cm across that open in the evening (finished by next morning) are produced from near the stem tips. This species will tolerate light to moderate frost.

REBUTIA

A group of free-flowering cacti that consists of about 40 species although many more names (including segregate genera such as *Sulcorebutia* and *Weingartia*) have been coined as a result of the great variation found within the genus and also because of their popularity in cultivation. Originating from mountainous regions of Bolivia and Argentina, these cacti are small-growers, mostly clumping, with compact stems bearing tubercles and neat clusters of spines. They are especially popular for their large colourful flowers that open widely during the day and last for several days. Well-grown plants often flower in mass, the flowers sometimes completely covering the plant and producing a spectacular display.

Generally easy to grow and relatively fast, these cacti do best in a container. Repot annually when young, then every two years. They need bright light (some tolerate full sun, others need protection from hot sun), good air movement and dry winter rest. Most will tolerate cold and frost, in fact some species grow much better in cold climates rather than milder sites. Increase by seed and careful division.

Rebutia albiflora

This Bolivian species sometimes produces so many flowers that the whole plant is completely hidden. It offsets freely to form a clump, the individual bright green cylindrical stems bearing groups of bristly white spines. Individual flowers are white with a pinkish caste.

Rauhocereus riosaniensis

Tony Wood

Rebutia albiflora

Rebutia arenacea

Tony Wood

Rebutia canigueralii subsp. *crispata*

Michael Mathieson

Rebutia canigueralii subsp. *pulchra*

Rebutia hybrid *(albiflora × heliosa)*

Tony Wood

Rebutia mentosa

Rebutia arenacea

A solitary or clumping species from Bolivia with small globe-like pale green to greyish stems, each with prominent tubercles. Bright yellow to orange flowers, each 2.5–3cm across, open widely on sunny days.

Rebutia canigueralii

An extremely variable Bolivian species with flower colour ranging from orange to red and pink to purple, sometimes with cream to yellow in the throat. It offsets freely to form a crowded clump, the flattish stems with distinct tubercles and pale bristle-like spines. The subsp. *crispata* has lovely purplish-pink flowers while subsp. *pulchra* has pale magenta or red flowers.

Rebutia hybrid (*R. albiflora* × *R. heliosa*)

Excellent for the novice grower, this vigorous hybrid quickly reproduces to form a crowded clump of globe-like stems. When flowering in spring and summer the plants carry red-brown buds that open widely to masses of delicate pinkish white flowers.

Rebutia mentosa

Although mostly offsetting freely to produce a crowded clump of flattish globose stems, solitary plants of this free-flowering Bolivian species are occasionally seen in cultivation. Lovely, purple to purplish pink flowers open widely on sunny days.

Rebutia perplexa

A clumping species from Bolivia that has very small globe-like to shortly cylindrical stems (each stem often less than 2cm tall and wide). The lovely mauve to lilac flowers, 2.5–3cm across, are usually larger than the stems.

Rebutia perplexa

Rebutia pseudodeminuta
Scarlet Crown Cactus

Native to mountainous areas of Bolivia at about 2500m alt., this popular species will form a crowded clump 10–15cm across. Individual stems are dark green with pale spines and the fiery red flowers (2.5–3cm across) with paler stamens produce an unforgettable display in spring and early summer.

Rebutia pseudodeminuta

Rebutia steinbachii

This variable Bolivian species (the variation is exemplified by its innumerable synonyms), embraces a range of growth forms and flower colours. Usually clumping and capable of fast growth, it develops a dense mound of small globe-like to shortly cylindrical stems. The clumps are at times so densely crowded that offsets become misshapen as they emerge. This species commonly has orange to red flowers but yellow and purple-flowered variants are known. The subsp. tiraquensis has numerous spirally arranged ribs, whereas subsp. verticillacantha lacks central spines. The four photos opposite illustrate some of the variation exhibited by *Rebutia steinbachii*.

Tony Wood

Rebutia steinbachii subsp. *verticillacantha*

Tony Wood

Rebutia steinbachii subsp. *tiraquensis*

Tony Wood

Rebutia steinbachii (the variant previously known as *Sulcorebutia mizquensis*)

Tony Wood

Rebutia steinbachii (the variant previously known as *Sulcorebutia krahnii*)

Rebutia xanthocarpa

Tony Wood

Sclerocactus uncinatus

Setiechinopsis mirabilis

Rebutia xanthocarpa

A clumping species from Argentina with flattish globe-like green stems 3–5cm across bearing groups of glassy spines. Carmine red flowers, each about 2cm across, produce an attractive display, sometimes forming a ring around the base of each growth.

SCLEROCACTUS

A genus of about fifteen species of cacti from southern USA and Mexico. Most are solitary, some clump. Stems range from globes to cylinders. The showy daytime bell-shaped flowers arise near the apex. Best grown in a container, these cacti, most of which are slow growers, need excellent drainage, bright light, good air movement and dry winter rest. Most will tolerate frost. Increase by seed or careful division.

Sclerocactus uncinatus Brown-flowered Hedgehog Cactus

Distributed in southern Texas and adjacent Mexico, this variable species is usually seen as a spiny bluish cylindrical column that can reach 20 × 12cm. The central spines are typically hooked and the flowers bell-shaped. Flower colour ranges from pink to red or brown, sometimes almost black. This species, which will tolerate frost, must be kept completely dry over winter. The subsp. *wrightiae* has fewer spines.

SETIECHINOPSIS

The single species in this genus has been included in *Echinopsis* until recent molecular studies supported its recognition as distinct. Although easily grown it is usually short-lived, lasting only a few years. Increase by seed.

Setiechinopsis mirabilis

An unusual cactus from eastern Argentina that develops a single dark green cylindrical stem 8–10cm tall and about 2cm thick. Clusters of short whitish spines are aligned in rows along the stems and decorative flowers arise near the stem apex. Each flower, which is carried on a furry floral tube 8–10cm long, has numerous narrow white petals. The flowers, which have a strong spicy fragrance, are easily missed because they open after dark and close before daybreak the next morning. A succession of flowers is produced over spring and summer, each followed by an elongated fruit containing an abundance of seed. Seedlings are easily raised, often flowering in their second year.

Stenocactus coptogonus

Tony Wood

Stenocactus crispatus

Tony Wood

Stenocactus crispatus

Tony Wood

Stenocactus crispatus

STENOCACTUS

About 10 species of popular Mexican cacti that can be recognised by globe-like stems with numerous prominent thin ribs that are often wavy. Mostly small and usually solitary (some clump with age), they have colourful striped flowers that open during the day (and last for several days). Generally easy to grow, but slow, these plants do best in a container. They need bright light (some tolerate full sun), good air movement and dry winter rest. Most will tolerate cold and light frost (flowering may be improved after a cold winter). Increase by seed or careful division.

Tony Wood

Stenocactus crispatus

Stenocactus coptogonus

Solitary or clumping, this attractive species has bluish green stems with ten to fifteen sturdy ribs that are mostly straight with transverse grooves across the front of each areole. Flowers, usually pale with a broad reddish purple midvein (but sometimes bright pink), open in spring. This species will tolerate light frost.

Stenocactus crispatus

An extremely variable cactus with numerous forms in cultivation; these are often grown under confusing names. The stems, which reach 8–12cm across, have strongly folded and wavy ribs. Lovely violet to purple flowers, the petals with a darker central band, open in late spring and summer.

Stenocactus multicostatus Brain Cactus

Plants of this cactus are usually solitary but sometimes clump with age (and when happy). Individual stems, 8–10cm across, are bright green and with numerous, closely spaced, narrow, wavy ribs in a brain-like pattern. Groups of colourful flowers (white with purple midveins) are well-displayed on the growth tips over spring and summer.

Tony Wood

Stenocactus obvallatus

Stenocactus ochoterenanus

Stenocereus alamosensis, flowers

Stenocactus multicostatus

Stenocactus obvallatus

A popular species, solitary (sometimes with paired stems) or clumping, with globose to cylindrical stems to 10cm tall. The stems are decorated with an unusual pattern of thin wavy ribs and sparse clusters of flat spines. White, cream or pale yellow flowers with prominent pink to red central bands are produced, mainly in spring.

Stenocactus ochoterenanus

Solitary or clustering, the bluish green globose stems of this species are well-armed with a mixture of projecting and spreading spines. White to pale pink flowers with darker central bands appear in spring and at intervals over summer.

STENOCEREUS

A genus of 23 species distributed from North America and the Caribbean Region to Colombia. They range from sprawling cacti with creeping stems to tree-like plants, all with spiny, ribbed, cylindrical stems. The funnel-like or bell-shaped flowers, mostly nocturnal (sometimes diurnal), sometimes remain open the next morning. These are mostly large or spreading cacti that need plenty of room to develop. Ideal in a semi-arid climate, they need good drainage, a sunny position and dry winter rest. Some will tolerate light frost. Increase by seed and stem cuttings.

Stenocereus alamosensis Octopus Cactus

In nature this Mexican species forms thickets of arching, heavily armed stems 1–2m long. Pot-grown specimens may need careful staking to keep them out of adjacent plants. Planted specimens are best isolated from other plants and may need judicious pruning to control their spread. Tubular pink to red diurnal flowers 8–10cm long are produced along the stems in summer. Interestingly the seeds of this cactus germinate in the fruit before it is shed.

Stenocereus beneckei

This species is from central Mexico, where it grows on rocky cliffs. It has a shrubby habit with arching to sprawling, slender, strongly tuberculate stems 1–2m long. Stem colour ranges from grey-green to reddish brown. Shiny brown buds 6–8cm long open at night to small white flowers that last into the next day. A desirable variant, which has the upper parts of the stems covered with a silvery-white powdery bloom, is grown by hobbyists. It is best kept in warm dry conditions and must be watered carefully and not handled as the bloom is easily rubbed off. Regular propagation of this selected variant by using stem cuttings taken from the top of a plant is necessary as the white surface gradually fades on the lower stem. This cactus will tolerate light frost only.

Stenocereus chrysocarpus

A large Mexican cactus (5–7m or more tall) with candelabra-like growth, the bright green upright stems arising from a sturdy trunk. Clusters of dark spines form rows along the ribs. White funnel-shaped flowers 6–8cm across, opening day and night, are followed by reddish purple fruit about 6cm long, each covered with bristles.

Stenocereus eruca Caterpillar Cactus, Creeping Devil

Both common names are apt for this viciously armed but slow-growing cactus that has creeping prostrate stems covered with dagger-like grey spines. The stems, 6–8cm across and up to 2.5m long, sprawl across the ground, often with the tips curving upwards. New parts root as they grow and the older parts die. Cream to pale pink flowers open at night. This unusual cactus is native to central parts of the Pacific coast of Mexico (Baja California Sur), where it forms large impenetrable colonies in sandy soil. It tolerates light frost only.

STETSONIA

The single species in this genus is a large cactus that is distributed naturally in north-western Argentina and adjacent arid areas of Bolivia and Paraguay.

Stetsonia coryne Toothpick Cactus

This large cactus forms a freely branching clump 5–8m tall and 2–3m wide. The pale green to bluish ribbed stems, 8–10cm thick, are formidably armed with long sharp spines. Scaly buds develop into large, white, funnel-shaped flowers. These impressive flowers, which

Stetsonia coryne

Stenocereus beneckei

Stenocereus chrysocarpus

Stenocereus eruca

open at night and often remain open the next day, are followed by green to reddish scaly fruit that have an edible skin with a citrus-like flavour. A sought-after crested form is grown by hobbyists. This species will tolerate light to moderate frost.

TEPHROCACTUS

Cacti in this Argentinian genus, which is a segregate from *Opuntia*, have jointed stems with globular or cylindrical segments. They also have sunken areoles and tufts of barbed spines (glochids) as well as normal spines. Colourful flowers are borne diurnally at the top of the stems, followed by dry fruit. Mostly easy to grow, but often avoided by hobbyists because of their relationship with *Opuntia*, they need sun, excellent drainage and an open position. Some will accept winter rainfall and most tolerate frost. Increase by seed or stem segments.

Tephrocactus articulatus **Paper-spined Cholla**

The most commonly grown form of this variable cactus (often known as var. *papyracantha*) has harmless papery spines that taper from a broad base. However, beware of the tufts of tiny barbed spines (glochids) that nestle at the base of the larger spines. Other forms are grown including the so-called var. *inermis* (Spruce Cone Cactus or Pine Cone Cactus) which has bumpy stems with glochids but no spines. Although easy to grow, this mostly frost-hardy species is very brittle and segments are easily detached by careless handling. White or yellow flowers are followed by dry barrel-shaped fruit.

THELOCACTUS

There are about twelve species of cacti in this genus, which is from south-western USA and Mexico, many growing in soils derived from limestone. Some are solitary, others form clumps. The colourful funnel-shaped flowers, which open during the day, are borne near the growth apex. Generally slow-growing, these globular to column-like cacti are usually grown in a container (garden-grown plants often split after taking up too much water). They need bright light (some in full sun), good air movement and dry winter rest. Some will tolerate cold, even frost. Sugary exudates from the areoles of these cacti can lead to the development of sooty mould. Increase by seed or careful division.

Paul Forster

Tephrocactus articulatus

Thelocactus bicolor Glory of Texas

Distributed in Texas and northern Mexico, this popular species is easily grown in a pot. Usually solitary, the plants, which can grow to 15cm tall, are well armed with colourful spines. Dark-centred magenta-purple flowers open freely on warm days in spring and summer. The subsp. *schwarzii* has very colourful flowers. This hardy species will tolerate frost.

Thelocactus conothelos

This species grows in the hills and mountains of Mexico between 800 and 2000m alt. Usually solitary, it forms a cylindrical growth 20–30cm tall and 10–15cm across. Colourful flowers in shades of pink, purple, yellow and orange (sometimes white) open widely on sunny spring and summer days. This species will tolerate light frost.

Thelocactus hastifer

Native to mountainous areas of Mexico at about 1900m alt., this clumping species (sometimes solitary) has pale green cylindrical stems 20–30cm tall with pale-coloured erect and spreading spines. Showy bright pink flowers are produced in summer and early autumn. This easily grown species tolerates light to moderate frost.

Thelocactus hexaedrophorus

A distinctive Mexican cactus which has flattish blue-green to olive-green stems with plump, rounded tubercles topped with stout spines. The large flowers (6–10cm across) are silvery white to silvery pink (sometimes with darker central bands). This slow-growing species will tolerate light frost.

Thelocactus macdowellii

Solitary when young but usually clumping with age, this Mexican cactus has a dense covering of white spines. Bright pink to magenta flowers about 4cm across are produced in winter–spring. This species will tolerate light frost.

Thelocactus tulensis

A variable species from hilly districts in Mexico between 800 and 1400m alt. The plants, which can be solitary or clumping, are variable in tubercle size, spination and flower colour (white to pink or magenta). The subsp. *matudae*, which has large tubercles and lovely bright pink flowers, is one of the best forms to grow. It will tolerate light frost.

Tony Wood

Thelocactus tulensis subsp. *matudae*

Thelocactus hexaedrophorus

Thelocactus bicolor subsp. *bicolor*

Tony Wood

Thelocactus bicolor subsp. *schwarzii*

Tony Wood

Thelocactus conothelos

Thelocactus hastifer

Tony Wood

Thelocactus macdowellii

Trichocereus bridgesii 'Monstrosa'

Trichocereus bridgesii, large clump

TRICHOCEREUS

A recent detailed study, based on both morphological and molecular data, has shown that *Trichocereus* should be reinstated as a distinct genus with *Helianthocereus* (those with colourful flowers) as a synonym. There are about 45 species of *Trichocereus* found in the Andes mountains of Ecuador, Peru, Bolivia, Chile and Argentina. They are columnar cacti which branch from the base to form a clump; overlapping scales along the tubular flower base; and fruit that are nearly round. Large fragrant flowers mostly open at night, with some lasting into the next day (sometimes two days if the weather is overcast). Mostly easy to grow, they need excellent drainage, good air movement and dry winter rest. Some will tolerate full sun, others respond to shade during the hottest part of summer days. Several species will tolerate cold, even frost, others need warmth. Increase by seed, division or stem cuttings.

Trichocereus atacamensis subsp. *pasacana*

Trichocereus atacamensis

In its native countries (Argentina, Bolivia and Chile) this massive columnar cactus is used as a timber resource for building dwellings, furniture and firewood. Growing 8–10m tall (but slowly) and with a large main trunk 50–70cm across, it presents an imposing spectacle. The strongly ribbed trunk is covered with reddish needle-like spines. Pinkish white flowers about 10cm across, borne laterally on the stems, are followed by followed by dark green densely hairy fruit that have a sweet edible flesh. The subsp. *pasacana*, from Argentina and Chile, branches more freely than the typical subspecies. It has been hybridized to a limited degree with other *Trichocereus* (particularly *T. formosa*). *T. atacamensis* subsp. *pasacana* will tolerate light frost.

Trichocereus bridgesii

A fast-growing columnar cactus that occurs naturally at high alt. in the Andes of Bolivia. This species forms clumps of pale green to somewhat bluish green stems

3–5m tall and 15cm across, each stem formidably armed with long spreading to drooping spines. White, fragrant flowers up to 20cm across open at night. A crested form is sometimes grown, as also is a novelty monstrose form known as the Penis Cactus or Penis Plant. *Trichocereus bridgesii* is very cold hardy, tolerating moderately heavy frosts. It also responds well to regular summer watering.

Trichocereus coquimbanus

A clumping species with a neat growth habit, the cylindrical stems to about 1m tall and 8cm thick covered with rows of short pale spines. Scented white flowers 12–15cm across open in the evenings in spring and summer, each flower lasting one or two days. Although from coastal parts of Chile, this species tolerates light to moderate frost.

Trichocereus formosus Pasakana Cactus

A clumping species from the Andes in Argentina and Chile. Barrel-shaped stems, to 1.5m tall and 50cm across, are covered densely with yellowish or reddish needle-like spines. Orange to red or yellow diurnal flowers, each 8–10cm across, are produced freely from the stem tips in spring and summer. This species has been used recently as a parent in some interesting crosses.

Trichocereus formosus, clump

Trichocereus coquimbanus

Trichocereus huascha, pale yellow

Trichocereus huascha, red

Trichocereus huascha, white

Trichocereus huascha, golden

Trichocereus hybrid (huascha × formosa)

Trichocereus pachanoi, flower

Trichocereus knuthianus

Trichocereus macrogonus

Trichocereus pachanoi

Trichocereus huascha
Torch Cactus

A very popular cactus that is prized for its displays of large colourful flowers (mostly shades of red but also white, pale yellow and a beautiful golden yellow form). Easily grown as a garden plant in a suitable position it forms clumps to 1m tall, the stems erect or reclining. Large flowers (6–10cm across) lasting two to three days open widely in the sun. This hardy species will tolerate full sun and most frost.

Trichocereus formosus

Trichocereus knuthianus

Native to Peru, this clumping cactus forms blue-green to grey-green column-like stems 2–3m tall. These stems have broadly rounded ribs and long spines (8–10cm) that can inflict painful wounds. Best in full sun and sited well away from paths, this species will tolerate light frost. Large white flowers are produced in summer.

Trichocereus macrogonus

The heavily scented flowers of this Bolivian species are truly spectacular. They open in the late afternoon–evening after the furry buds have grown to about 18cm long and swollen impressively before bursting. The flowers themselves are snowy white and up to 25cm across. Sometimes appearing in pairs or small groups, they pervade the whole area with their fragrance, especially on warm humid nights. The stems, which can reach 2.5m tall and 10cm thick, have a grey green to bluish caste. This hardy species will tolerate full sun and most frost.

Trichocereus pachanoi San Pedro Cactus

This commonly grown columnar cactus, native to Ecuador and Peru, has a clumping or tree-like habit with stems to 5m or more tall and 10–15cm across. The bluish to dark green stems, which are cylindrical and mostly without spines, are deeply furrowed. Fragrant white flowers 15–20cm across arise near the stem tips and open on summer nights, usually finishing the next day. The tubular base of each flower

Trichocereus schickendantzii

Trichocereus scopulicola

Trichocereus smrzianus

Trichocereus spachianus

is covered with black scales and curly hairs. This species will tolerate moderately heavy frost. It also responds well to regular summer watering. Recently this species has been reduced to a variety of *T. macrogonus*.

Trichocereus schickendantzii

An excellent cactus for a pot or the garden with the plants developing into a clump of crowded column-like stems to 25cm tall. Although this Argentinian species forms an attractive clump, its flowers (about 12cm across) are by far its most notable feature. The buds are red with black hairs and the nicely scented diurnal flowers open white with pink to red tones in the outer segments. This species, which will tolerate light to moderate frost, needs a cold winter to initiate flowers.

Trichocereus scopulicola

A tall clumping cactus that has thick, mostly spineless, blue-green, column-like stems 3–4m tall. Clumps of woolly hairs on the stems develop into large funnel-shaped white flowers (15–20cm across) that open in the evening (summer), each lasting about one day. Easily grown, this Bolivian species will tolerate light to moderate frost.

Trichocereus smrzianus

Usually seen growing as a dense clump of slender prickly stems ranging in height from 10–20cm tall, this species, which is from northern Argentina, can also consist of a solitary stem 30–40cm tall. Lovely white flowers 12–15cm across, which open during a warm summer evening, usually last well into the following day.

Trichocereus spachianus White Torch Cactus

This popular cactus, native to western Argentina, forms crowded clumps with column-like stems 1–2m tall. Yellowish to lime green stems are covered with rows of yellow spines. Magnificent snowy white scented flowers, each to 20cm long and 15cm across, are produced at intervals during spring and summer lasting one or two days. This hardy species will tolerate full sun and most frost.

Trichocereus thelogonus, clump

Trichocereus thelogonus

Tony Wood

Turbinicarpus horripilus

Trichocereus thelogonus

An interesting cactus that crawls across the ground, the stems, which can reach about 2m long, covered with needle-like yellowish spines. Large funnel-shaped flowers with pointed petals (outer segments greenish, inner snowy white), 12–15cm across and produced from near the stem tips, open during summer evenings. This species will tolerate light to moderate frost.

TURBINICARPUS

These cacti are popular with hobbyists for their compact habit and colourful flowers. Consisting of about 24 species, these Mexican cacti usually grow in areas where limestone or gypsum predominate (some growers add 10% gypsum to the potting mix). They are usually solitary (some clump with age) and the diurnal flowers arise near the growth apex in spring and summer. Generally slow growing, these cacti are sometimes grafted to improve the growth rate. Best in a container, they need excellent drainage, bright light (some in full sun), good air movement and dry winter rest. Some will tolerate cold, even light frost, others need warmth. Increase by seed or careful division.

Turbinicarpus horripilus

One of the faster-growing species that will sometimes clump with age. Mature stems, which are usually only about 5cm across, have wool on the young areoles and prominent spines. Lovely purple flowers make this species a favourite with growers.

Turbinicarpus lophophoroides

This species, which grows naturally in gypsum-rich soil, can retract underground during the dry season, emerging again following substantial rain. It is solitary with a flattened globose blue-green stem 3–5cm across. The younger areoles have prominent

Turbinicarpus lophophoroides

tufts of white wool (shed with age) and showy white to pink flowers appear from the top of the plant in late summer–autumn. Being prone to rot this attractive species is often grafted.

Turbinicarpus valdezianus

A slow grower with a solitary stem that appears silvery white due to a dense covering of white feather-like spines. White to pink or magenta flowers with darker midveins produce an impressive display in spring. This species needs bright light, to avoid elongation, and careful watering, to prevent rotting.

Turbinicarpus viereckii

Growing naturally in rock crevices, this species demands excellent drainage and careful watering. It can clump with age, the small spiny stems having white woolly tops. White to bright pink flowers are produced in late spring and early summer.

Tony Wood

Turbinicarpus valdezianus

Turbinicarpus viereckii, photo Tony Wood

The large colourful flowers of *Epiphyllum* hybrids appeal to growers

Part Three
GROWING EPIPHYTIC CACTI

Because many aspects of the cultural requirements of epiphytic cacti differ from those of terrestrial cacti they are dealt with here as a separate group. Basically epiphytic cacti have similar cultural requirements to other epiphytic plants, especially orchids. For notes on housing cacti in general see page 30.

THE APPEAL OF EPIPHYTIC CACTI

Epiphytic cacti have a group of dedicated followers within the cactus-growing fraternity. Epiphytic cacti are faster growing than their terrestrial relatives and are well suited to developing as specimen plants within a relatively short time. They offer a range of unusual growth habits that are themselves appealing to hobbyists – the unusual leaf-like stems supplemented by appealing floral displays, and sometimes also with masses of colourful fleshy fruit. Many have large flamboyant orchid-like flowers which modern hybridists have interbred to produce a wide range of bright colours. Some of the nocturnal flowerers have perfumes so deliciously fragrant that they enhance the night atmosphere with pleasant scents. Some have short-lived flowers that appear in succession over several weeks, others are much longer lasting. Careful selection can provide flowers over much of the year; consider for example the popularity of the autumn–winter flowering zygocacti (*Schlumbergera*) and the spring-flowering *Epiphyllum* hybrids (strictly *Disocactus*).

NATURAL HABITATS

Epiphytic cacti originate in the tropics where they grow naturally on trees and rocks in forests (often but not always in rainforest). People associate the tropics with heat, high rainfall and high humidity; however, not all tropical areas have the same climate. Some areas have rain evenly spread throughout the year (and few or no epiphytic cacti); whereas others, where epiphytic cacti proliferate, have a strongly seasonal climate with distinct wet and dry times. The wet season (termed 'the wet'), which is a time of heavy rainfall, high temperatures and high humidity, is followed by a dry period (termed 'the dry'). In the dry time, rainfall is very low or non-existent for several months, and cooler temperatures and lower humidities prevail. Often the forest trees in these areas shed a high proportion of leaves in the dry season (or become completely leafless), allowing bright light to pass through the canopy.

Many epiphytic cacti originate in seasonal tropical climates. Cultivated plants benefit from a resting period (usually corresponding to winter) when they are kept drier than in the summer when they grow actively.

TEMPERATURE

Most epiphytic cacti are sensitive to cold and can be damaged or killed by frost. Those from lowland tropical areas are especially cold sensitive and begin to suffer when temperatures fall to 8°C. Altitude considerably modifies tropical climates and as a general rule those species originating from high mountains in the tropics are more tolerant of cold, although they may still need protection from frost. Epiphytic cacti from subtropical zones are less cold sensitive than the tropical ones but can still suffer frost damage.

HUMIDITY

Humidity is a reflection of the water vapour present in the atmosphere. It is also closely linked with temperature. Thus at low to moderate temperatures, high humidities are much less noticeable than they are at high temperatures. Unlike their terrestrial cousins, epiphytic cacti need moderate levels of humidity for normal growth and development, although they can withstand some fluctuation. It is difficult to maintain a constant high humidity and a level of about 50% is usually quite satisfactory for a general collection. Humidity can be increased by watering, misting and the use of humidifiers.

VENTILATION AND AIR MOVEMENT

Good air movement is a major factor in the successful cultivation of epiphytic cacti. It distributes oxygen, carbon dioxide and water vapour around the plants, prevents stagnant conditions and reduces the incidence of pests and disease. Air movement should be gentle, either induced by successful ventilation or by the use of internal fans. Excessive air movement dries out plants.

LIGHT AND SHADE

Epiphytic cacti prefer bright but diffuse light similar to that which would be filtered through a leafy tree canopy. This diffuse or filtered light is especially important over summer as these plants can bleach or burn quite badly if exposed to too much hot summer sun.

PHOTOPERIOD

The hours of daylight received is known as the photoperiod. The length of the photoperiod (or more accurately the length of the dark period) plays a major role in stimulating the flowering of epiphytic cacti. Long-day species, such as *Epiphyllum* hybrids, respond to decreasing periods of darkness (increasing daylength), whereas short-day species are the reverse. Some tropical species may be unresponsive to photoperiod.

SUITABLE CONTAINERS

Epiphytic cacti are commonly grown in hanging pots or baskets because most of these plants have a pendulous habit that can be displayed to effect in this type of container. Drainage holes of pots should be cleared or enlarged before use. Hanging baskets are especially popular for some groups, such as *Rhipsalis* species Wire hanging baskets have been traditionally used, but these are giving way to plastic baskets. Wire baskets must be lined to retain the potting mix. Suitable materials include sphagnum moss, staghorn peat, paperbark and coconut fibre. Precut fibrous basket liners are also available. A wide range of plastic baskets is available, but only those with excellent drainage are suitable. Basal saucers should be removed for epiphytic cacti as they can impede drainage and retain excess water during heavy rain. Hanging baskets, especially wire baskets, generally dry out rapidly, particularly in windy weather, and more frequent watering will be needed.

POTTING MATERIALS

Epiphytic cacti must be potted into a coarse organic mix through which water passes rapidly to be replaced by air. Growers use either commercial orchid mix or good quality potting mix, but avoid cheap brands which often have too much fine material that can clog up the pores. Products of this type are based on softwood bark (pine or redwood). The best bark (used in quality orchid mixes), which has a nuggety or flaky texture (the worst bark is stringy), is from large mature trees and is available in a range of sizes (grades). Fresh bark, especially with a strong resinous smell, may contain toxic materials that can inhibit root growth and should be treated by storing wet in a heap for about six weeks. Suitable softwood barks have a pH of 6–6.5. The pH of pine bark is initially about 5 but rises with age to 6.5.

POTTING COMPOSTS

Numerous potting composts are used by growers, depending on the availability of materials. A useful basic mix can be prepared by mixing equal parts orchid bark or good quality potting mix and coarse sand or perlite. Do not add lime as epiphytic cacti need an acid mix. Some growers add vermiculite, chopped sphagnum moss or coconut fibre to increase the water-holding capacity. Other materials, including

Rhipsalis pachyptera in basket

Hatiora rosea in hanging pot

charcoal, peanut shells and chunks of coconut husk can also be added. Gravel, perlite and polystyrene are useful for keeping a mix open, thus ensuring good aeration and providing a safeguard if the mix breaks down. Gravel is heavy and may sink in a mix, whereas the other materials are lighter, but they tend to float to the surface after watering. Potting mixes should be moistened or soaked before use because some material can be very difficult to re-wet if used in a dry state.

POTTING AND REPOTTING

It becomes necessary to repot epiphytic cacti when:

- the potting mixture begins to break down, impeding drainage and reducing aeration; the presence of moss, algae or persistent weeds on the surface of the mix is a useful guide to deteriorating potting mixes
- the pot/basket is so full of roots and the mixture exhausted of nutrients that growth is suffering
- the pH of the mix becomes unsuitable (usually too acid) for root growth (sometimes this can happen within one or two years of potting)
- the plant outgrows its container (see also under Potting On)
- the mix is unsuitable for local conditions; this often applies to purchased plants or those obtained from other growers

TIMING: Repotting is best carried out in the warmer months (spring is the best time), especially just after flowering. Autumn and winter are not a good time for repotting epiphytic cacti unless it is the only way that a plant can be saved.

POTTING PROCEDURE

- Before repotting dry the plant out for a week or so to facilitate removal from the pot.
- Tip the plant from the container, remove most of the old potting mix, eradicate any pests such as slaters and earwigs, and trim off any dead or damaged plant tissue (roots, stems).
- Place the trimmed plant in the new container and fill firmly with potting mix to support the plant. Settle the mix by tapping the base of the container on a bench. Ensure that the potting mix is level with the base of the plant without burying any new stems. Some growers fill the pots to the rim, others leave a catchment of 2–3 cm to aid watering.

Epiphyllum 'Lavender Marshmallow'

- Stake any plants that have a poor root system to prevent excessive movement until new roots are produced. Label immediately and place the newly potted plant in the growing area.

POTTING ON

This is the simple procedure of moving an established plant into a larger container without greatly disturbing the roots. It is only employed for strong-growing plants in which the potting mix is still in good condition (no deterioration). Fill any gaps with new potting mix.

WATERING EPIPHYTIC CACTI

Watering needs vary depending on temperature, light intensity, wind and rainfall. Outdoor plants dry out more rapidly than those in a greenhouse. Epiphytic cacti have high water requirements when in active growth over the warmer months (late spring to autumn), but need much less water when quiescent in late autumn and winter. Even when in active growth, however, most epiphytic cacti are well adapted to withstand moderate periods of dryness. In summer (tropics and temperate regions) water every one to four days. Water much less in temperate regions in winter, about every 10–15 days (even in a greenhouse). In the tropics water every three to five days in winter.

Watering should not be confused with misting or damping down which is carried out to enhance humidity. Watering consists of thoroughly drenching the root system until excess water flows out the drainage holes. This prevents the build-up of mineral salts which can damage the roots. Some growers prefer to water early in the morning, others in the evening. The time of watering is probably unimportant in the summer months, but morning watering in the winter is best, allowing time for the plants to dry out.

FEEDING EPIPHYTIC CACTI

Epiphytic cacti benefit from feeding during spring and summer when in active growth. Late feeding may delay dormancy, reduce the tolerance of plants to cold weather and interfere with flowering. Organic fertilisers, such as blood and bone, are excellent for epiphytic cacti because they release nutrients in a slow and sustained manner. Aged or composted animal manures can also be successful. Slow-release fertilisers are modern alternatives which some growers use, but they can lead to root loss from salt buildup. They can either be incorporated when potting or added during the growing season. Liquid fertilisers are an excellent means of maintaining healthy growth. Commercial mixtures are available and some growers prefer to concoct their own. Organic extracts such as fish emulsion and seaweed extracts promote root growth and are popular with growers. Specialised fertilisers (such as those used by orchid growers) designed to enhance plant growth or flowering are often used by dedicated growers of *Epiphyllum* hybrids. Be guided in their use by local growers and seek information at society meetings.

PESTS AND DISEASES

A general treatment of cactus problems is included in part two (pages 33–38). Epiphytic cacti suffer from attacks by mealy bugs and scale insects. The soft new growths can also be devoured by slugs and snails. They also suffer leaf rots which can be controlled by Anti Rot.

PROPAGATING EPIPHYTIC CACTI

Epiphytic cacti are easily propagated by stem cuttings taken in the warmer months after flowering. Whole stem sections 15–20cm long (with a basal junction area) are ideal for *Epiphyllum* hybrids whereas smaller sections are used for *Aporophyllum*, *Hatiora* and *Schlumbergera*. Allow the cutting to dry for seven to ten days before potting into sandy propagating mix (equal parts sand and potting mix works well). Rooted plants can be potted when they show signs of growth. Epiphytic cacti can also be raised from seed or used in novelty grafts (for more on propagation see pages 39–45).

Disocactus nelsonii

EPIPHYTIC CACTI TO GROW

DISOCACTUS

There are sixteen species of *Disocactus*, most occurring in Central America, with others in the Caribbean and northern parts of South America. Mostly pendulous, they exhibit significant variation in growth including two species with slender spiny stems that are circular in cross-section (both were previously placed in *Aporocactus*). Most *Disocactus* have ridged or flattened leaf-like stems. The colourful flowers open during the day. Few species are grown in Australia. Ideal subjects for a hanging basket, they need excellent drainage, winter dryness and, as a general rule, protection from frost.

Disocactus ackermannii

Native to Mexico, this is one of the most commonly grown species. Popular for its ease of growth and large colourful flowers, it can be grown in a shadehouse, under trees or on a sheltered verandah. Usually seen in a hanging basket, it can also be successful in a tub or even planted in the ground in the sandy soil of sheltered coastal gardens. Plants grow to about 1m tall, the flattened stems branching freely.

Disocactus ackermannii

Disocactus ackermannii fruit

The main display of green-centred scarlet flowers, each 12–16cm across, occurs in late spring, with occasional flowers opening during summer and autumn.

Disocactus eichlamii

This spineless Guatemalan species forms a graceful clump with flattened secondary stems arising from arching to pendulous circular primary stems. The narrow flattened stems, from which the flowers arise in late spring and early summer, have indented margins. Pink funnel-shaped flowers 8–10cm long arise along the shoots (sometimes in groups), opening in succession.

Disocactus flagelliformis Rats-tail Cactus

A popular Mexican species that is ideal for a hanging pot or basket. The slender terete stems, which can reach 1m long (but only 15–20mm across), are covered in pale spines (mostly reddish yellow). The plants branch freely and in spring produce lovely purplish-pink upward-facing flowers 3–5cm across that last several days. A specimen plant produces an impressive floral display, the flowers mostly concentrated towards the basal part of the stems. This species will tolerate quite heavy frost and full sun. A cristate form is much prized by collectors.

Disocactus × hybridus

This is a man-made primary hybrid between *Disocactus phyllanthoides* and *D. speciosus*. It has erect to arching ridged and flat leaf-like stems and lovely scarlet flowers that are strongly funnel-shaped. It grows readily in a hanging pot or basket.

Disocactus × hybridus

Disocactus eichlamii flowers

Disocactus eichlamii

Disocactus flagelliformis flowers

Disocactus flagelliformis in basket

Disocactus macranthus

Disocactus macranthus

Disocactus martianus

Disocactus macranthus

A distinctive species from Mexico that forms a much-branched bushy clump of slender pale green flattened stems with notched margins. Young plants have upright stems but older plants spread or hang. Starry flowers 3–5cm across open in autumn when few other epiphytic cacti are out. The flowers, which have a pleasant fragrance, are cream to pale yellow (brownish yellow with age) with a central group of white stamens.

Disocactus martianus

Although similar in general appearance to *D. flagelliformis*, the terete stems of this Mexican species are covered in dark brown spines. It is also more robust, the stems recorded as reaching more than 4m long. This species, which does not produce the spectacular floral displays of *D. flagelliformis*, has scattered red funnel-shaped flowers 10–12cm long in spring.

Disocactus nelsonii

Adaptable in temperate regions, although still requiring protection from severe frost, this species forms a dense clump of dark green fleshy leaf-like stems. Widely opening bright pink flowers 5–7cm across are a pleasant surprise when they appear in spring (sometimes also in summer). An excellent basket plant, with large specimens producing massed floral displays, this species originates from high alt. forests in Mexico.

Disocactus nelsonii

Disocactus phyllanthoides

An old-time spring-flowering favourite from Mexico that can be difficult to grow well (it favours morning sun and performs best in coastal areas). It forms a bushy clump (to 1 × 1m) of light to dark green flattened leaf-like stems. Pink flowers 5–7cm across have the outer segments spreading widely, while the inner segments form a tube around the stamens. In this species the buds develop slowly, the bracts separating early to impart the impression of miniature flowers.

Disocactus speciosus

This Mexican species has ridged and flat leaf-like stems that become pendulous with age. Stem margins have spiny areoles and attractive funnel-shaped flowers 8–12cm across open in late spring. These are bright red with a whitish or bluish caste. This species, which is very sensitive to frost, needs to be displayed in a hanging container.

Disocactus phyllanthoides flowers

Disocactus phyllanthoides

Disocactus speciosus

DISOCACTUS (APOROPHYLLUM) HYBRIDS

These *Disocactus* cultivars are commonly but mistakenly known as *Aporophyllum* hybrids. Most commonly they are the result of crossing the larger-flowered *Disocactus* hybrids (popularly called Epiphyllums – see next entry) with the commonly grown Rats-tail Cactus (*Disocactus flagelliformis*). Until fairly recently this species was known as *Aporocactus flagelliformis* and, as a result, the hybrids are still commonly called '*Aporophyllum* hybrids'. They have slender prickly stems that that are round to angular in cross-section and arch or dangle freely to form a pendulous clump. They produce colourful flowers 5–8cm across in the spring, usually earlier than the bulk of *Epiphyllum* hybrids. The flowers, which arise on the older stems, mostly last two to four days. These hybrids are generally slow-growers and can be more difficult to establish than their larger cousins. They need very good ventilation and brighter light to flower successfully. Mealy bugs establish readily in the axils where stems branch and can also become established at the base of flower buds, growing rapidly as the buds increase in size.

Aporophyllum 'Edna Bellamy'

Aporophyllum 'Cascade'

Aporophyllum 'Slim'

Aporophyllum 'Marie'

Aporophyllum 'Sarah'

DISOCACTUS (EPIPHYLLUM) HYBRIDS

This group of hybrids is the result of many years of complex hybridisation. The original crosses probably involved several genera of epiphytic cacti, especially *Disocactus*, *Epiphyllum* and *Selenicereus*, with the resultant hybrids also backcrossed to various species. The modern crosses are mainly between the hybrids themselves, with limited backcrossing to some species. Mostly these hybrids form large clumps consisting of narrow to broad stems that are mainly flat and leaf-like, but some are winged or variously ridged. Some hybrids have upright stems, others arch and become pendulous with age, while a few dangle from the outset.

There are hundreds of *Epiphyllum* hybrids (if not more) available in a huge range of flower colour and flower size. Frequently called 'Orchid Cacti' because of their spectacular flowers (but this name is also shared with zygocacti), they flower in late spring and early summer. Flower size ranges from about 10cm wide to flamboyant blousy giants 20–30cm across. The flowers, which can be incredibly beautiful, unfortunately only last one or two days; large well-grown plants can produce a display over several weeks.

Hybridisation in this group is a continuing but rather haphazard process. Planned breeding by crossing selected parents with desirable traits (including growth features such as vigour and habit as well as floral features) may well produce some really spectacular progeny. Currently this approach is not apparent and there are many hybrids that share more similarities than differences. Culling the progeny to weed out weak-growers should also be a priority. As a further problem there is also much confusion as to the correct hybrid names used between and within countries. Apart from these minor drawbacks these plants are well worth growing and have a dedicated following of growers in many countries.

Cultivation: These popular cacti can be grown in a hanging basket on a sheltered verandah, under established trees or in a shadehouse. Filtered light is best, but a position exposed to morning sun can be successful. Protect from frost. Water frequently from spring to autumn then less frequently to harden plants for winter. Keep much drier over winter but do not allow the stems to shrivel. Feed regularly over summer. Apply sulphate of potash in July–August to help flower initiation. Repot every two to four years to maintain vigour. Prune off straggly growths or those that have been damaged by frost or fungus disease. Reddish plants have either too much sun or a damaged root system. Avoid handling plants in bud as the buds are easily dislodged. Cuttings 20–25cm long establish well but smaller pieces can also be successful. Slugs and snails relish the soft growth of these plants and can quickly devastate a season's growth.

Epiphyllum 'Great Walz'

Epiphyllum 'King Midas'

Epiphyllum 'Sweet Prince'

Epiphyllum 'Mystic Mood'

Epiphyllum 'Patrician'

Epiphyllum 'Kemsley of Kent'

Epiphyllum 'Agatha'

Epiphyllum 'Bohemienne'

Epiphyllum 'Ulana Lemon Bitters'

Epiphyllum 'Calisto'

Epiphyllum 'Dainty Lady'

Epiphyllum 'Ulana Lavender Giant'

EPIPHYLLUM

All nineteen species of this Central American and South American genus are clumping epiphytes with flattened leaf-like stems and showy flowers (mostly white) that open at night. The flowers of some species remain open for a couple of days; others only last one night. These cacti are easily grown, especially in warm tropical areas. Many make very decorative basket plants. They need frost protection and limited watering over winter (but not complete dryness.

Epiphyllum anguliger

Epiphyllum anguliger
Moon Cactus

In Mexico, the Gooseberry-like fruit of this cactus is eaten as food. In many other countries the plant is grown as a popular basket subject where it is valued for its decorative lobed stems and scented flowers. The flowers, which are carried on long floral tubes, have narrow white inner segments surrounded by pale yellow to golden outer segments.

Epiphyllum crenatum

This is a vigorous species that is native to Mexico, Guatemala and Honduras. It is variable with one variant (var. *crenatum*) forming a clump upright of pale green stems 6–10cm wide, whereas the more commonly grown var. *kimnachii* has widely spreading dark green stems to more than a metre long, but only 4–6cm wide. The stems of both varieties, which are flattened and leaf-like, have bluntly scalloped margins. Large fragrant flowers (15–20cm across) that last one to three days are produced from apical areoles in late spring and early summer. The flowers, carried on long floral tubes, are mainly cream or white with the outer segments tinged with green, pink or brown.

Epiphyllum crenatum var. *crenatum*

Epiphyllum crenatum var. *kimnachii*

Epiphyllum oxypetalum plant

Epiphyllum oxypetalum

Epiphyllum pittieri plant

Epiphyllum pittieri

Epiphyllum oxypetalum Queen of the Night

This widely distributed Central American species is easily recognised by its thin-textured leaf-like stems with wavy margins. The secondary and tertiary stems, shorter than the long main stems (which are round in cross-section), often spread at right angles and impart a very distinctive growth pattern to the plant. Large cupped flowers (15–20cm across) with broad inner segments and narrow outer segments (often pinkish) open on summer nights. Unfortunately these lovely flowers last but a single night, fading quickly the next morning.

Epiphyllum pittieri

Small plants of this Central American species are erect, but with age the flattened stems arch and droop, eventually growing 2m or more long. They are dark green with shallowly scalloped margins but can take on bronze tones in winter. Starry white flowers 3–5cm across, with intriguing narrow tepals, open on warm nights in early summer (sometimes also later in the season), the flowers lasting a single night.

Epiphyllum pumilum

Cutting-grown plants of this lovely species start off by forming a clump of fairly thin-textured flattened stems which have sparsely toothed margins and long-pointed tips. When well-established the plants then extend outwards by producing runner-like stems 2–3m long with side shoots towards the apex. Trimming these long shoots early in their development helps keep the plants compact and away from others. Creamy white fragrant flowers about 6–8cm across open during warm summer and autumn nights, often lasting well into the next day. This species, which is native to Mexico, Guatemala and Belize, needs shade and can bleach badly if exposed to excessive light and sun.

Epiphyllum pumilum fruit

Epiphyllum pumilum small plant

Epiphyllum pumilum

Hatiora gaertneri 'Scarlet Triumph'

Hatiora gaetneri

HATIORA

Two species in this small Brazilian genus of five species are popular in the USA where they are known as 'Easter Cacti', because their flowering period coincides with that religious time. Inexplicably this common name has carried over into Australia, despite them flowering in late spring over here. Three species are commonly grown in Australia. They are bushy plants with stems either flattened or terete and developing in short segments. Growth is initially erect and the stems arch or spread in older plants, becoming pendulous in *H. salicornioides*. The trunk-like basal stems eventually thicken and become quite woody. Flowers, mostly large and colourful, develop on the ends of previous years stems. They are radially symmetrical (actinomorphic), which contrasts with the zygomorphic flowers of the similar and often confused genus *Schlumbergera*. Species of *Hatiora* are valued for their neat growth, spineless stems and colourful floral displays. They are easily grown in a hanging pot or basket of epiphyte mix in shade or semi-shade in a well ventilated site protected from frost. They need regular watering as the roots can die if they become too dry (plants wilt badly), but they can also suffer root rot if overwatered. They also respond to misting on hot sunny days.

Hatiora gaertneri specimen plant

Hatiora gaertneri

In nature this handsome species grows among the clouds at about 2000m alt. in the mist forests of the Mantiquiera mountains of south-eastern Brazil. It forms a large clump with whorls of arching dark green stems to 30cm long. Brilliant displays of bright red to deep scarlet flowers produced on the end of the branches in October–November always attract attention.

Hatiora rosea

This species grows on trees in semi-deciduous forests in the mountains of south-eastern Brazil, near the border with Uruguay. It has a very bushy habit, the narrow concave stems branching freely. Lovely pale pink to deep pink flowers appear at the growth tips in late spring. A limited range of selected forms (or possible hybrids) are grown by collectors.

Hatiora rosea 'Collette'

Hatiora rosea 'Pink Pixie'

Hatiora rosea 'Regina'

Hatiora rosea 'Springtime'

Hatiora rosea 'Sweet Song'

Hatiora rosea, pale pink variant

Hatiora salicornioides Drunkard's Dream

An intricately branched species that forms arching or hanging clumps up to 1m long. The short fleshy stems, which are club-shaped (or perhaps better described as bottle-shaped), are green in shade but take on pink to reddish tints in sun. Bright yellow to orange flowers, 1–2cm long, adorn the stem tips in early spring. This species, one of the easiest epiphytic cacti to grow, is an ideal plant for the beginner.

HYLOCEREUS

These cacti, which are true epiphytic climbers, have no need for contact with the ground, their stems being supported by strong aerial roots. The stems are angular, often three-lobed in cross-section, with the outer parts expanded as flattened wings and the margins scalloped or lobed. They are capable of ascending the trunks and larger branches of tall trees. Many species are too vigorous for general cultivation but could find a home in tropical gardens. The large funnel-shaped flowers (mostly white, sometimes red) open at night, usually lasting just one or two days. If pollinated they are followed by unusual fleshy fruit that are covered with large scales. Some species, such as Dragon Fruit, are grown commercially in the tropics for their edible fruit.

Hylocereus undatus Dragon Fruit

Although usually seen growing in the tropics, where it is commonly planted for its large tasty fruit, this species has proved to be quite adaptable and can be grown in frost-free coastal areas of south-eastern Australia. Plants can reach 4-5m tall, but when grown for fruit, they are better confined to a manageable size by regular pruning. The showy white flowers (15–20cm across) appear at intervals from spring to autumn. Cross-pollination between flowers ensures fruit set. Commonly the large ovoid succulent fruit (8–12 × 5–9cm) are red when ripe, but yellow and white forms are also grown.

LEPISMIUM

This genus consists of seven species of epiphytic cacti from South America, particularly Bolivia. Popular with hobbyists, the genus includes a number of pendulous species with slender stems that look appealing when grown in a hanging container. Some exhibit variation in growth form, adding to their appeal to collectors. Once established they can accept some dryness (but not too dry). Protect from frost and keep on the dry side over winter. Prune to shape if necessary.

Hatiora salicornioides flowers

Hatiora salicornioides

Hylocereus undatus plant

Hylocereus undatus

Lepismium cruciforme flowers

Lepismium cruciforme

Lepismium houlletianum

Lepismium houlletianum

Lepismium cruciforme

This is a wonderfully decorative plant for any hanging container, especially a basket. Large plants can grow more than 1m long, the intricately branched and crowded stems often taking on red or purplish tones in bright light. Widely distributed in Argentina, Brazil and Paraguay, it is variable in stem shape (flat or angularly winged), flower size and flower colour (cream, yellow, pink or purple). The form most commonly grown has three- to five-angled red to purple stems that are prominently winged. Pink flowers open in spring, each flower subtended by a tuft of silky white hairs that persist after the flower dies. Globose fruit, 5–10mm long, are red or purplish when ripe.

Lepismium houlletianum

A vigorous Brazilian species (perhaps also from Bolivia) that forms large bushy clumps, sometimes more than 2m long and 1m wide. Mostly pendulous, it sometimes sends out thin stems 1–2m long that develop groups of flattened stems at the apex (great for propagating). The flattened stems, which are thin and leaf-like, have coarsely toothed margins (sometimes reddish). White bell-shaped flowers 1.5–2cm long add interest to the plant in late winter-spring (and sporadically at other times). These are followed by small red to black fruit. Although easily grown in a large hanging pot or basket, this species can be susceptible to nutritional problems, particularly iron and magnesium deficiencies. The stems can also bleach or burn in excessively bright light.

Lepismium warmingianum

An excellent basket plant with narrow drooping stems that have numerous aerial roots. The stems, which can be flat or angular, have bluntly toothed margins. Pendulous bell-shaped white fragrant flowers 1.5–2cm long produce an attractive spring display, often developing from consecutive areoles at

Lepismium warmingianum

the stem tips. The flowers are followed by small round black fruit that can persist for some months. This South American species (Brazil, Paraguay and Argentina), which occurs up to 1100m alt., will tolerate light frost.

PFEIFFERA

Recent molecular studies have shown that this genus, which consists of six species, is distinct from *Lepismium* where they were previously placed (they have also been placed in *Acanthorhipsalis*). These cacti, which are found in Bolivia and northern Argentina, have a shrubby habit with erect to pendulous, flattened or ribbed stems that are often spiny and lack adventitious roots. Most are easy to grow and look appealing in a hanging container. They need filtered light or semi-shade and good ventilation. Once established they accept some dryness. Protect from frost and keep on the dry side over winter. Prune to shape if necessary.

Pfeiffera monacantha

Easily grown and relatively tolerant of cold, this species, native to the mountains of Bolivia and Argentina at 500–2000m alt., forms much branched clumps of spreading to pendulous, flat or angular spiny stems with toothed margins. Orange flowers 12–15mm across, produced from areoles on the upper parts of mature stems are followed, by round pink to orange fruit that persist for many weeks. Well-grown plants can produce a colourful display of flowers and fruit over many months.

Pfeiffera paranganiensis

Originating from the area of Cochabamba in Bolivia at about 3000m alt., this species adapts well to cultivation and is relatively tolerant of cold, including light frost. Small plants have stiffly upright spiny stems but older plants, which can grow 2–4m long, are usually pendulous. Creamy white to yellowish flowers 1.5–2cm across appear in groups towards the tips of mature stems. Globose to top-shaped fruit about 1cm long are brownish when ripe.

Pfeiffera monacantha flowers

Pfeiffera monacantha fruit

Pfeiffera paranganiensis

Lepismium houlettianum, flowers

Rhipsalis baccifera flowers

Rhipsalis baccifera

Rhipsalis campos-portoana flowers

Rhipsalis campos-portoana

RHIPSALIS

Avidly collected for their range of intriguing growth habits and sculptural form (but often difficult to identify with certainty), these epiphytic cacti grow naturally in seasonal forests where there is a distinct dry season that can extend over weeks and months. The genus contains about 35 species, including a number that exhibit a range of variation in growth form, adding to the appeal for collectors. Many of these growth variants are in cultivation in Australia and it seems apparent that some of the plants grown here have been wrongly identified. These cacti are mostly from tropical America (particularly Brazil) and the Caribbean region, with *R. baccifera* extending to islands in the Indian Ocean. Mostly with a pendulous or hanging habit, these plants are best grown in suspended containers where their special appeal can be appreciated. Being adaptable, they can be grown with care and shelter in temperate regions, but are easiest in warmer frost-free climates, especially coastal districts and the subtropics. Once established they accept some dryness. All are frost sensitive but many are surprisingly cold tolerant if given some protection (tree canopy or verandah) and watered very sparingly (if at all) over winter. Prune to shape if necessary.

Rhipsalis baccifera Mistletoe Cactus

This species is the most widely spread member of the genus, extending from South and Central America and the Caribbean to Madagascar, tropical Africa and east as far as Sri Lanka. It exhibits significant variation over its range, with six subspecies recognised. The growth habit of this easily grown species is variable, but most forms branch sparingly and have an open habit with short stiffly spreading branches. Some forms grow upright, others arch or hang. Small widely opening whitish flowers (5–10mm across) in winter and spring are followed by translucent white to pinkish fruit 6–8mm long.

Rhipsalis campos-portoana

A wonderful basket plant that is very easy to grow, forming a bushy pendulous clump that can eventually reach 2–3m long. The thin (2mm wide) light green stems branch regularly to form a series of overlapping whorls. Well-grown plants flower freely in spring, the white bell-shaped flowers, each 8–10mm long, providing a nice display and contrasting with the green stems. These are followed by small bright round orange or yellow fruit.

Rhipsalis cereoides

This species grows naturally on gneissic rocks in eastern Brazil from sea level to about 900m alt. It forms straggly clumps consisting of erect to arching, thick, three- to four-angled, dull green stem segments. White flowers about 2cm across, borne singly or in groups of up to four, open in spring. Globose fruit about 4mm across can be white or pink when ripe. This species, which is very slow growing, needs warm conditions in winter.

Rhipsalis cereuscula Coral Cactus

A commonly grown species that is widely distributed in the forests of South America (Bolivia, Paraguay, Uruguay, Brazil and Argentina). The plants, which can be straggly or bushy, form pendulous clumps to more than a metre long. Stems of two different types are present giving the species a unique appearance; long slender pencil-like stems arch from the main clump and then develop clusters of short crowded angular stems. Often small bristles are prominent on the new growth of this species. White or pinkish bell-shaped flowers 1–1.5cm across in spring are followed by small white fruit. This easily grown species is a good plant for the beginner.

Rhipsalis clavata

The short stem segments of this pendulous Brazilian species are produced in crowded whorls so that a large plant develops a very bushy habit. It is an excellent subject for a basket or other hanging container, with large plants growing to about 1m long and of similar width. The short stems, which thicken prominently towards the tip, are usually bright green and shiny but can become reddish in bright light. Bell-shaped white flowers about 1.5cm long are followed by small round white fruit.

Rhipsalis cereoides

Rhipsalis cereuscula flowers

Rhipsalis cereuscula

Rhipsalis clavata

Rhipsalis crispata flowers

Rhipsalis crispata

Rhipsalis elliptica

Rhipsalis ewaldiana flower

Rhipsalis crispata

This Brazilian species, which has flat leaf-like stems with attractively scalloped margins, can be slow and difficult to start, but grows steadily once established. It forms a straggly clump 20–40cm long, the stems spreading to hanging. Starry white to yellowish flowers about 1.5cm across appear in spring in groups up to four from the grooves that separate the leaf crenations. They are followed by small white spherical fruit. This species, which occurs naturally in strongly seasonal forests, needs very careful watering in winter.

Rhipsalis elliptica

Native to Brazil where distributed from lowland forests to mountainous areas at about 2000m alt., this species often grows upright when young but forms sprawling clumps with age. A handsome plant, it is characterised by broad segments (to 7cm wide) that narrow to the base and with blunt marginal teeth. Prominent buds jutting out from the leaf margins in autumn open to an attractive display of white or yellow fragrant flowers. These are followed by small red fruit.

Rhipsalis ewaldiana

Known only from cultivated plants, this Brazilian species forms a sprawling, much-branched clump 50–60cm long and of similar width. The slender stems, which are three- to four-angled, are dark green in shade but much paler and with reddish tints in bright light (and when undernourished). White flowers, produced freely in spring, are followed by spherical rosy pink fruit.

Rhipsalis ewaldiana

Rhipsalis floccosa

A variable species (with six subspecies recognised) that is widely distributed in the moist lowland forests of many South American countries, including Brazil, Venezuela, Argentina and Paraguay. The plants, which branch freely, are erect at first and then hang. They have sturdy terete stems (4–8mm across in the various subspecies) with darkened areas around the areoles. Smallish flowers (10–15mm across), sometimes fragrant, ranging from white to greenish or golden yellow and with the base nestling in a tuft of wool, are produced freely in spring. Spherical fruit follow ranging from white to pink or red. The subsp. *hohenauensis* is especially distinctive with its yellow buds opening to white flowers.

Rhipsalis goebeliana

Native to Bolivia, this species forms sprawling or dangling clumps to about 1m long. The flat, dark green, leaf-like segments, about 3cm wide, have bluntly lobed and somewhat wavy margins. Each segment, which is thin-textured with a thickened central vein, tapers to a narrow base. White flowers (about 1cm across) are produced along the stem margins in autumn. Established plants of this very decorative species look particularly appealing in a hanging basket. It attains it best appearance in shade or filtered light.

Rhipsalis grandiflora

This Brazilian species is characterised by chubby cylindrical stems 12–15mm thick and branches arising in whorls or by forking at steep angles from the main axis. It extends from rocky coastal sites to forests above 1000m alt. and has showy cream to white flowers about 2cm across that open widely in autumn–winter. It is an excellent basket plant that prefers dim light or shade and protection from all but light frost. Shade-grown plants have dark green stems, whereas those in bright light can take on reddish tones, with the region around the areoles (which have no bristles in this species) pigmented with red or purple. The somewhat flattish rounded fruit, 6–8mm across, ripen purple.

Rhipsalis floccosa subsp. *floccosa*

Rhipsalis floccosa subsp. *hohenauensis* buds and flowers

Rhipsalis floccosa subsp. *hohenauensis* fruit

Rhipsalis goebeliana

Rhipsalis grandiflora flowers

Rhipsalis grandiflora

Rhipsalis hoelleri

Rhipsalis megalantha flowers

Rhipsalis hoelleri

A poorly known species from lowland forests of Brazil that forms a dangling clump 1–2m long. The dark green stems (3–4mm diameter.) are round in cross-section and bright pink to scarlet flowers, about 10mm across when fully open, with contrasting white stamens burst through the epidermis. Small globose fruit are bright red when ripe.

Rhipsalis megalantha

This species has a growth habit similar to *R. grandiflora* but with ribbed yellow-green stems with dark areoles and large scars where the flowers/fruit have been. The flowers, which can be even larger than those of *R. grandiflora* (to 4cm across), are cream to yellowish. This species is also less tolerant of cold, especially frost than many other *Rhipsalis*.

Rhipsalis mesembryanthemoides

Distinctive within the genus, this novel Brazilian species is readily recognised by the numerous short (1–2cm long) side branches (actually secondary stems) that are packed together along the much longer primary stems. This imparts a crowded or bushy appearance to the plant. Small plants are mostly erect but the primary stems (10–20cm long) of older plants spread or hang. White flowers about 1.5cm across are followed by small white fruit.

Rhipsalis mesembryanthemoides

Rhipsalis micrantha

This species, which is widely distributed in South America (Costa Rica, Venezuela, Colombia. Ecuador, Peru) growing from sea level to about 2000m alt., exhibits considerable variation. Several variants are probably in cultivation. Two forms of quite different appearance make excellent hanging basket plants. *Rhipsalis micrantha* forma *micrantha* has narrow (5–7mm wide) flat or slightly angular stems 50–60cm long without marginal teeth. It branches freely from the stem tips to produce a fairly narrow hanging clump. Its white flowers are about 6mm across. By contrast, *R. micrantha* forma *rauhiorum* has shorter stems (8–12cm long) that also branch freely from the stem tips. The stems however are wider (1.2–2cm), often with two or three ridges, and have prominent blunt teeth along the margins. It forms a pale green to bright green bushy clump to 1m long and 30–70cm wide. White flowers about 1cm across, are followed by translucent, greyish to whitish egg-shaped fruit 6–8mm long. A straggly very frost-sensitive plant (see photo), may be another variant of this species. A distinctive form with broad arching stems is grown in the USA. Its stems have scalloped margins and new stems are produced from areoles towards the base of a mature stem (not from the stem apex as in other forms).

Rhipsalis neves-armondii

This Brazilian species, which forms similar crowded clumps to those of *R. grandiflora*, is characterised by thick stems produced in whorls, with darker clearly defined areoles that have short bristles, cream to white flowers about 2cm across and red globose fruit about 1cm across. It grows well in a hanging pot or basket forming a dangling much-

Rhipsalis hoelleri, flowers

Rhipsalis micrantha, straggly form

Rhipsalis micrantha forma *rauhiorum* fruit

Rhipsalis micrantha forma *rauhiorum*

Rhipsalis paradoxa subsp. *septentrionalis*

Rhipsalis neves-armondii flowers

branched clump with a pleasant appearance. Frost damage, even from a light frost, shows up as dieback of the stem tips.

Rhipsalis pachyptera in basket

Rhipsalis occidentalis

A widespread species from humid highland rainforests of Peru, Ecuador and Suriname. It forms a clump to 1m long of dangling bright green stems (often shiny) with the individual stems 5–7cm wide and narrowing to the base, and with strongly scalloped margins. White flowers about 1cm across, singly or in pairs from the areoles, are followed by white fleshy fruit 7–8mm long. This easily grown species needs more shade than most *Rhipsalis*.

Rhipsalis pachyptera

A wonderful basket plant that originates from low alt. rainforest in Brazil where it grows on rocks and trees. It has broadly flattened leaf-like stems 10–12cm wide and branches freely to form clumps up to 1m long, the main stems pendulous with the side stems spreading widely. Individual stem segments, which are thick and flat, have scalloped margins where small (15–20mm across) white to yellowish strongly fragrant flowers appear in spring. Although dark green in shade, this frost-sensitive species takes on reddish tones in sun and can become deep purple when grown hard.

Rhipsalis paradoxa Chain Cactus

Although its stems can grow 3–5m long, cultivated plants of this Brazilian species are usually shorter. It is readily recognised by the short, three to four-angled stem segments, each 15–20mm across, that are linked to produce a slight zigzag or chain-like effect. The light green, limply hanging stems branch sparsely and when long enough produce white flowers (20mm across) near the segment tips (although this species seems to be a very shy flowerer). Spherical pinkish fruit follow. Planting several struck cuttings together and tip pruning from an early age produces a bushier and more attractive plant. The subsp. *septentrionalis* (commonly called the Link Cactus) has much thinner stems than the typical subspecies and is reported

Rhipsalis occidentalis

Rhipsalis pachyptera flowers

Rhipsalis paradoxa subsp. *paradoxa* stems

Rhipsalis paradoxa subsp. *paradoxa*

Rhipsalis pentaptera

Rhipsalis pilocarpa forma *minima*

Rhipsalis pilocarpa forma *minima*

Rhipsalis puniceodiscus flowers

to have yellow flowers. Its stems also hang limply but the chain-like appearance is not as pronounced.

Rhipsalis pentaptera

This Brazilian species has an arching habit with the stems branching freely and spreading widely to form a bushy clump to 80cm long and wide. It is easily identified by the four to six ribs that run along each stem. White flowers about 1.2cm across are followed by small white or pink fruit. Although easy, this species is generally slow growing.

Rhipsalis pilocarpa Mouse Tail Cactus

The hairy stems of this easily grown Brazilian species appear white when backlit by strong light. A vigorous clumper that is excellent as a basket plant, its stems arch from the base and branch freely at the tips where they often develop a cluster of numerous short stems. Plump buds carried at the end of each stem open in winter as attractive flowers 3-4cm across that are white with a red centre. The small round red fruit are covered with bristle-like spines. *Rhipsalis pilocarpa* forma *minima* has a more compact growth habit and smaller flowers (1.5cm diameter) that lack the red centre.

Rhipsalis puniceodiscus

A robust Brazilian species that forms a large bushy pendulous clump 2–3m long. Each stem branches freely developing whorls of dark green pencil-like stems (3–5mm thick) with numerous aerial roots. White flowers 15–20mm across with a prominent red central patch of stamens open at intervals throughout the year. The fruit are commonly pink to red, although yellow-fruited forms are known. A dark scar remains on the stems where a fruit has developed. This easily grown species, which looks best in shade, will tolerate light frost.

Rhipsalis puniceodiscus

Rhipsalis teres Mop Tops

Several variants of this variable Brazilian species are in cultivation. The typical form develops into a bushy clump about 60cm long and 40cm wide. It has cylindrical stems 3–5mm thick that develop whorls of new stems at the apices. Young plants often grow upright at first before spreading and becoming pendulous. An ideal basket specimen, it forms a dense more or less rounded clump of bright green to yellowish stems. White or cream flowers about 1.2cm diameter are followed by small white globose fruit. The forma *capilliformis* has wiry stems only 2–3mm thick. A distinctive bushy variant – forma *prismatica* – has short, angular, hairy branches that sometimes appear to be almost square in cross-section.

Rhipsalis trigona

This easily grown Brazilian species forms a pale green to bright green much-branched bushy clump to 2m long and 80cm wide. The pendulous stems, which are distinctly three-angled, branch at the tips. Shiny brown buds open in winter–spring to fragrant white or pinkish flowers 2–2.5cm across. Egg-shaped fruit 6–8mm long are red when ripe.

Rhipsalis teres forma *capilliformis*

Rhipsalis teres forma *teres* fruit

Rhipsalis teres forma *teres*

Rhipsalis teres forma *prismatica*

Rhipsalis trigona

Rhipsalis trigona flowers

SCHLUMBERGERA ZYGOS, ZYGOCACTUS, CRAB CACTUS

There are about six species in this genus of Brazilian epiphytes, which are probably better known by their old generic name of *Zygocactus*. Nowadays the original species have been largely replaced in collections by a series of modern hybrids. Easily the most commonly grown of all cacti, these distinctive plants are propagated annually in their thousands in many countries. They are popular for their general ease of growth and colourful floral displays (large old plants can produce hundreds of flowers each year). They can also be long-lived with cherished specimens passed on between generations. In Australia these cacti flower in late autumn and winter, but in the USA their habit of flowering in December has earned them the common names of Christmas Cactus, Thanksgiving Cactus and Holiday Cactus. They also share the name of Orchid Cactus with *Epiphyllum* hybrids and are sometimes called Crab Cactus or Crab's Claw Cactus because of the shape of individual stem segments.

Schlumbergeras have flattened stems (or phylloclades) that replace leaves. They are arranged in short determinate sections, are green and can photosynthesise. The margins have teeth, either short and blunt, or protruding and softly pointed (the stem often looks jagged), the apical pair of each section often resembling a crab's claw. The areoles (containing tiny bristles) occur on the stem margin in the notch formed where each tooth arises. Large showy flowers, mostly zygomorphic (except for *S. russelliana*) are often followed by smooth or angular, pink to red, fleshy, ovoid fruit.

Schlumbergera russelliana

Schlumbergera russelliana

Distinguishing features of this species include short blunt lobes on the stem segments and regular (actinomorphic) flowers with pink pollen. An excellent basket plant with pendent or hanging stems, it is often the last in the group to flower.

Schlumbergera truncata

This species can be recognised by the pointed tooth-like lobes on the margins and tips of the stem segments and the strongly zygomorphic flowers with white pollen. It is a vigorous grower that with care can become a cherished long-lived plant.

Schlumbergera × *buckleyi*

This is a primary hybrid between *Schlumbergera russelliana* and *S. truncata* that may occur in the wild. It has narrow stems with shallowly rounded lobes on the margins and pinkish-red flowers. This hybrid is vigorous and easy to grow.

Schlumbergera × *buckleyi*

Schlumbergera truncata

SCHLUMBERGERA HYBRIDS

The original *Schlumbergera* species have bright pink to reddish flowers, but nowadays hundreds of cultivars are available in a wide range of colours. The array of these plants is extensive and sometimes the differences between cultivars are difficult to discern. Shades of pink and red predominate the colour range but white-flowered cultivars are also known and 'yellows' – more pinkish with cream to yellow hues rather than bright yellow – are prized. Attractive bicoloured cultivars are also popular. The lineage of many *Schlumbergera* hybrids is unrecorded.

Cultivation: These popular cacti are easily grown but a few pointers may improve results. Unlike most epiphytic cacti, *Schlumbergera* need a rest period in January–February. Water carefully to keep them moist, but don't overwater or allow them to become excessively dry. The plants must also be treated carefully after flowering, as the effort of flower production seems to drain the plant and they can appear as if 'exhausted'. It is untrue that these cacti must be potbound and starved to flower well. Feed over summer (but rest January–February) and repot every three to five years to maintain vigour. Some growers prune the outer two stem sections off their plants in August to encourage compact growth and branching.

Sick plants, which become limp and reddish, have generally lost their root system, usually as a result of overwatering or (less commonly) from drying out due to lack of water. Do not water affected plants but tip them out and examine the roots –white roots are healthy; soft brown roots have died or rotted. Take cuttings to save the cultivar. Use Anti Rot to control root rot. Plants in bud should not be moved to minimise bud drop. Flower colour may not be consistent from season to season and may vary noticeably even within a single plant. Propagate from stem sections taken in spring and summer. Single stem sections can be successful (not the top section as it is often too soft) but pieces with two or three sections of growth are better (larger cuttings can also be successful). Allow to dry for a few days then pot into a sandy propagating mix. Repot cuttings when showing growth.

Schlumbergera 'Christmas Fantasy'

Schlumbergera 'Christmas Cheer'

Schlumbergera 'Millenium Fantasy'

Schlumbergera 'Carol'

Schlumbergera 'White Christmas'

Schlumbergera 'Savannah'

Schlumbergera 'Kimberley'

Schlumbergera 'Madison'

SELENICEREUS

This genus, comprising 28 species of night-flowering cacti, includes climbers with cylindrical to angular stems and epiphytes with flattened leaf-like stems. Distributed from southern parts of the USA and the Caribbean region to South America, they are grown mainly by hobbyists. The flowers, which are often fragrant, are followed by spiny, fleshy fruit. Although easy to grow, these tropical cacti can be shy to flower. They need warm humid conditions and no frost.

Selenicereus anthonyanus climbing a tree

Selenicereus anthonyanus Rick Rack Cactus

Although this species has similar fishbone-like stems to those of *Weberocereus imitans*, the two are readily distinguished by their very different flowers. The Rick Rack cactus, which gets its popular name from its zigzag stems, has widely opening, starry flowers with narrow petals, the few inner white ones contrasting with the numerous pink to reddish outer segments. Also an excellent basket specimen, this Mexican species needs bright light to flower well.

Selenicereus chrysocardium Fernleaf Cactus

Prized for its long drooping decorative fern-like stems, this popular Mexican species makes an excellent basket plant, but is also grown as a novelty climber in tropical gardens. The flattened bright green stems, which can reach 1m or more in length and 30cm width, are divided nearly to the midrib into numerous tapered lobes. Large cupped flowers with an unusual smell (sour cream) arise from the upper axils. Each flower (16–20cm across), which has a long reddish basal stalk, is white, with a conspicuous central patch of gold stamens. This species needs shade or filtered light and winter warmth.

Selenicereus anthonyanus

Selenicereus grandiflorus

Robert Funnell

Selenicereus chrysocardium

Robert Funnell

Selenicereus chrysocardium

Selenicereus grandiflorus

Another species that is frequently known as the 'Queen of the Night'. This cactus has long, more or less cylindrical stems that climb or thread through surrounding shrubs and trees. Each stem, which can grow 3–5m long, is green with small, short-lived, bristle-like spines. Spectacular long-stalked flowers open on late spring or early summer evenings. Each flower, which can be 20–25cm across, has a central cup of broad overlapping white petals surrounded by numerous, narrow, tan to pale yellow segments that spread widely. This interesting species can be grown through garden shrubs, trained on a fence, or grown in a large hanging basket.

Selenicereus grandiflorus

Selenicereus megalanthus Yellow Pitaya

A South American climber that branches profusely to form a scrambling clump 2–3m long. The narrow dark green stems, 4–6cm across, are three-angled with scattered groups of short spines along the ribs. Fragrant, nocturnal, cream to white funnel-shaped flowers 20–25cm across (with narrow greenish outer segments) are followed by knobby yellow fruit that contain edible flesh. Spines are shed from ripe fruit allowing the tangy flesh to be easily appreciated. This tropical species is easily killed by frost.

Selenicereus grandiflorus in basket

Selenicereus megalanthus fruit

WEBEROCEREUS

There are nine species in this genus of epiphytic cacti, mainly from Central America, with one species in northern South America. They are clumping or climbing cacti, with arching round or flattened leaf-like stems and aerial roots. The flowers, which arise on the upper stem margins, open on summer nights. A single species is grown in Australia.

Weberocereus imitans

Native to the rainforests of Costa Rica, this handsome species forms a clump of bright green spreading to pendulous leathery stems which are deeply lobed like a fishbone fern. Cream, bell-shaped flowers (with a green base), 6–7cm, long, 3–4cm across, have an unusual smell. Although a shy flowerer, this species makes a very decorative basket specimen. It needs shade or filtered light and winter warmth.

Weberocereus imitans

Schlumbergera 'Gold Fantasy'

Glossary

actinomorphic said of flowers that are symmetrical and regular in form; the flower can be bisected symmetrically in several planes (cf. zygomorphic)

aff., affinity a botanical reference used to denote an undescribed species closely related to an already described species

anther the pollen-bearing part of a stamen

appressed pressed closely against the stem

areole a specialised bud on a cactus stem that produces spines and flowers

armed with spines

articulate jointed, divided into segments (as in *Opuntia* stems)

axil the upper angle formed by a leaf or branch with the stem

axillary borne within the axil

barbed with projecting hooks

berry a fleshy many-seeded fruit that does not split when ripe

bisexual both male and female sexes present

bract a leaf-like structure on a stem or supporting the ovary of a flower; it lacks a blade or lamina

calcareous of soil having an excess of lime

calyx all of the sepals of a flower

CAM stands for crassulacean acid metabolism, a respiration cycle found in most succulents, including cacti

candelabra-like describing a growth habit where many erect stems arise from a central trunk

central spines the innermost spines of a cluster (these often project forwards); see also radial spines

cephalium a specialised area on the stem where flowers arise; usually indicated by masses of woolly hairs or bristles which completely hide the stem

cladode flattened stem or stem segment that resembles a leaf

clone a group of plants propagated vegetatively from one plant (usually a superior form); all members of a clone are genetically identical

clumping, clustering with many stems growing from a common base

columnar column-like, applied to the stems of some cacti

creeping growing along the ground, prostrate

crest, cristate an abnormal fan-like development of a stem

cross-fertilisation fertilisation by pollen from another flower

cross-pollination transfer of pollen from flower to flower

cultivar a horticultural variety of a plant or crop

cylindrical in the form of a cylinder

deciduous falling or shedding of any plant part

decumbent growing along the ground with the stem tips raised

deflexed abruptly bent downward

dehiscent splitting open when ripe

dimorphic existing in two different forms
dioecious bearing male and female flowers on separate plants
distichous arranged in two opposite rows.
endemic restricted to a particular region, country or area
entire whole; not toothed, lobed or divided in any way
epiphyte a plant that grows on other plants but does not parasitise them
exotic a plant introduced from overseas
family a taxonomic group of related genera
floral tube basal portion of the corolla that is fused to form a tube
floriferous free-flowering
fruit the seed-bearing organ developed after fertilisation
genus a taxonomic group of closely related species
germination the active growth of an embryo resulting in the development of a young plant
glaucous covered with a bloom or powder to give a bluish lustre
globose globular, almost spherical
glochid tiny barbed spine found in the *Opuntia* group of cacti, often present in tufts
habitat ecological locality where the plant occurs naturally
hybrid the progeny of a cross between two species, cultivars or other hybrids
hybridisation the act of crossing flowers to produce hybrids
indehiscent not splitting open at maturity
indigenous native to a country, region or area
inflorescence the flowering structure of a plant (the flower stem and all the flowers)
juvenile the young stage of growth before a plant is capable of flowering
lateral arising at the side of the main axis
latex milky sap produced from damaged parts of some cacti; some species of *Mammillaria* for example
lithophyte a plant growing on rocks
lobe a segment of an organ resulting from division
marginal attached to or near the edge
medium the potting mix in which a plant is grown; the mixture on which seeds are raised
midrib the principal vein that runs the full length of a leaf, leaflet or petal
monstrose abnormal development resulting from the growth of multiple growing points
naturalised introduced from another area and able to compete with local vegetation
nectar a sweet fluid secreted from a nectary
nectary specialised structure that produces nectar
node a point on the stem where leaves or bracts arise
offset a basal growth produced from the side of a main stem
ovoid egg-shaped in a solid plane
pectimate comb-like
pendent hanging downwards
perianth a collective term for all the sepals and petals of a flower

petal a segment of the inner perianth whorl or corolla

phylloclade another term for a cladode

podarium outgrowth of the stem surface; tubercle

pollen the one-celled male spores borne in the anther

pollination the transference of pollen from the anther to the stigma of a flower

prostrate lying flat on the ground

pseudocephalium an area on the stem where flowers are produced but differing from a true cephalium in bearing lateral flowers from hairy areoles with the stem ribs still visible

radial spines the outermost spines of a cluster (these often radiate outwards); *see also* central spines

recurved curved backwards

seed a mature ovule containing an embryo and capable of germinating

segment part of an organ

sepal a segment of the calyx or outer whorl of the perianth

sessile without a stem or stalk

simple undivided, unbranched; of one piece

species a taxonomic group of closely related organisms with a common set of characters that sets them apart from another group

spination collective term for the spines of a plant

spine a greatly modified leaf; in cacti a stiff sharply pointed structure arising from an areole

stem segment a part of a stem separated by a constriction

stem succulent a succulent with thickened stems for water storage (most cacti are stem succulents)

stigma the enlarged sticky area that terminates the pistil, is receptive to pollen and allows the pollen grains to germinate

subspecies a taxonomic subgroup within a species used to differentiate geographically isolated variants

succulent fleshy or juicy; a plant capable of storing water in swollen roots, stems or leaves

synonym another name for the same taxon; either an alternative name valid in a different classification system or an invalid or incorrect name

taproot thickened carrot-like root

taxon a term used to describe any taxonomic group, for example genus and species

tepal used for perianth segments of a flower when the sepals and petals are alike

undulate wavy

variegated where the base colour of a petal or leaf is broken by areas of another colour

variety a taxonomic subgroup within a species used to differentiate variable populations

vegetative asexual growth or propagation

xerophyte a plant adapted to survive in regions of low rainfall

zygomorphic said of a flower that can be divided into two similar halves in one plane only (cf. actinomorphic)

Further Reading

Anderson, E.F. (2001). *The Cactus Family*, Timber Press, Oregon.

Anderson, M. & Hewitt, T. (consultant) (2008). *The Complete Illustrated Guide to Growing Cacti and Succulents*, Lorenz Books, London.

Chance, L.J. (2012). *Cacti and Succulents for Cold Climates*, Timber Press, Oregon.

Ellis, J. (2007). *The Cacti Handbook*, D & S Books, England.

Hewitt, T. (1993). *The Complete Book of Cacti and Succulents*, Dorling Kindersley, New York.

Innes, C. & Glass, C. (1991). *The Illustrated Encyclopaedia of Cacti*, Simon & Schuster, East Roseville.

Schuster, D. (1984). *Cacti in Australia*, Thomas Nelson, Melbourne.

Süpplie, F. (1990). *Rhipsalis & Lepismium*, The EPRIC Foundation, The Netherlands.

Epiphyllum 'Acapulco Sunset'

Epiphyllum 'Clarence Wright'

Acknowledgements

Many people have fostered my interest in cacti over the years and most have contributed in one way or another to this book. Special thanks go to the late John Spencer of Goulburn. John, with his excellent collection of cacti and succulents, was always willing to share plants and pass on his knowledge. Much appreciation also goes to Jim, Julie and John Hall of Cactus Country in Strathmerton, Victora, for showing Barbara and I around their wonderful collection, allowing us to take photographs, passing on bits and pieces of treasured cacti, and sharing hard-earned knowledge. Similar thanks to the Bevan family of Lighning Ridge for allowing us access to their well-established collection. Kath Carter has always been especially generous allowing me full access to her well-grown collection, passing on snippets and sharing plants.

In the special world of epiphytic cacti I say many thanks to Ted and June Clapson for their hospitality, and for opening my eyes to this fantastic group of plants, and generously sharing treasures from their collection. My daughter Sandie shares my fascination for these plants and on many occasions has negotiated the perils of Sydney driving on my behalf in the pursuit of new treasures. I also thank Tony Hanson for his marvelous 'Ulana' series of *Epiphyllum* hybrids, as well as passing on hints on hybridising and seed raising.

Again Paul Forster deserves a special mention. Paul made a significant contribution to my earlier book, *Starting Out With Succulents*, and again has been very generous with his time, answering numerous botanical queries, checking photographs for accuracy, reading much of the text and supplying a number of photos. Tony Wood, Barbara Jones and Miriam Nauenburg also commented on parts of the text.

Most of the photographs are mine but several others made contributions. I thank Tony Wood for his lovely shots of flowering and potted cacti; Paul Forster for some interesting shots, especially those taken in the wild; Michael Mathieson for photographing some of Paul's collection; the late Ron Tunstall for photographs of grafted cacti; and Robert Funnell for the photos of *Selenicereus chrysocardium*. Graham and Di Waldon gave me access to their flowering plant of *Selenicereus grandiflorus*, and Barry and Judy Roberts to their *Hylocereus undatus*. Catherine Jordan located obscure publications that benefited the text. Others, including Greg and Alice Daniels, Phyllis Collins, Lyle Felippe, Lester Meyers, Steve Pincott, Terry

Tierney and Fiona Webber, are thanked for various contributions.

Again my thanks to Fiona Schultz, Lliane Clark and Diane Ward at New Holland Publishers for their support, and especially to Jodi De Vantier for her patience in answering my numerous queries as well as her editing skills.

Finally very special thanks my loving wife Barbara, who puts up with my interest in cacti and has accompanied me on visits to various cactus collections and shows. Barb, although not so keen on cactus prickles, really appreciates the beauty and variety of their flowers.

Trichocereus smrzianus after rain

Index

Epiphyllum 'Andromeda'

First published in 2013 by New Holland Publishers
Sydney

Level 1, 178 Fox Valley Road, Wahroonga, NSW 2067 Australia

newhollandpublishers.com

A record of this book is held at the National Library of Australia.

ISBN 9781921517198

Managing Director: Fiona Schultz
Project Editor: Jodi De Vantier
Designer: Kimberley Pearce
Photographs: David L. Jones and others where specified
Photo opposite title page: Paul Forster
Production Director: Arlene Gippert
Printed in China

10 9 8 7 6 5 4 3

Keep up with New Holland Publishers
NewHollandPublishers
newhollandpublishers